TRUSTING TO LEARN

TRUSTING TO LEARN

THROUGH AN UNWANTED ANSWER TO PRAYER

A MEMOIR

BY EILEEN KUSAKABE

Printed in the United States of America

Published by Author Academy Elite
P.O. Box 43, Powell, OH 43035
www.AuthorAcademyElite.com

The author has recreated events, locales, and conversations from her memories of them. Some names and identifying details have been changed to protect the privacy of individuals.

Paperback ISBN 978-1-946114-68-6
Hardcover ISBN 978-1-946114-69-3
Ebook ISBN: 978-1-64085-338-6

Library of Congress Control Number: 2017906282

Author Academy Elite, Powell, OH

Cover design by Estella Vukovic
Cover photo by Asa Ellison

To Jim,
Thank you for allowing me to quit my paying job to write, and for loving me through so many seasons.
I love you.

To Brandon, Kylie, and Noah,
Owen,
Elyse and Ryan,
Thank you for all the joy you bring.

To Jesus,
Thank you for life.

The LORD says, "I will guide you along
the best pathway for your life.
I will advise you and watch over you."

—Psalm 32:8 (NLT)

CONTENTS

FOREWORD

As an unbelievable risk-taker, my friend and colleague Eileen Kusakabe gave her all to the Lord, anticipating his blessing. Instead, his response brought an unwelcome and life-changing trial. Her memoir of choosing to trust God's difficult plan offers an unusual perspective on God's incredible love.

Eileen explains her thought process throughout the journey and reflects on other odd answers to prayer throughout her lifetime. As much a confession of past failures as a profession of her faith, here the value of walking with Christ is richly portrayed. One can see God's hand upon her life despite shortcomings and poor choices early on.

As the plot unfolds, Eileen gives up her expectations of who God is and how to please him, and her heartfelt cry receives its answer. The uniqueness of God's voice in Eileen's life and the dreams in which he reveals his plans can only be attributed to the greatness of Jesus Christ. Submitting to God has forever altered Eileen, and her obedience to share her story is a blessing to enjoy.

Although unfathomable to us humans, *Trusting to Learn* reveals how God can use the ugliness in life for his glory. I highly recommend this book, and it is my great privilege to have been a part of its inception and ultimate completion.

Kary Oberbrunner,

CEO of Redeem the Day and Igniting Souls.
Author of *Elixir Project, Day Job to Dream Job, The Deeper Path,* and *Your Secret Name*

PROLOGUE

Opening the rusty door of our rural mailbox, I pulled out the day's offering of grocery ads, preapproved credit card applications, and appeals for donations to save the world. With a sigh, I leafed through the stack, stopping on a thin-papered envelope. Its foreign postage and solicitor's return address made my pulse quicken as time slowed.

Can this be it? Can this be the provision God told me to ask for? (Weeks earlier, I'd received notice of a supposed inheritance from a distant relative that I'd met but once.)

Nah, it can't be. I frowned, shaking my head. *Things like that only happen in Disney movies.* Tearing open the envelope, pulling out the single sheet it bore and reading its message, I felt a smile spreading across my face.

The brief, friendly letter mentioned an amount of an unknown currency due to me. Hurrying to our old computer, I punched the number into Google's currency converter and laughed aloud at the result. God had indeed answered my prayer. Not only had he sent a year's salary, he'd added a small raise!

My dear husband, Jim, standing outside watering his beloved plants with a long, dirty green hose, looked up as I bounded over to him. Letter in hand, I proclaimed, "I am going to quit my job."

"No, you're not."

I held it open in front of his face. "Do you know what this means?"

"Nope, not a clue." He glanced at the document and turned away, shooting the hose into another potted plant.

Glancing left and right I whispered, "It's over thirty thousand dollars!"

"Whoa!" He gave me a wide-eyed smile. "That's terrific, but it's not enough for you to retire."

My arms flopped to my sides as my head fell to my chest. I took a deep breath and asked, "When you're done, can we talk?"

"Sure." He shrugged, then dragged the hose to a new spot.

Sitting at the dining table, tapping my foot, I soon heard the squeak of the faucet as Jim turned the water off. He opened the back door, wiped his feet, and then sat in the chair facing me. "What's all this about?"

"Jim, this inheritance is a direct answer to my prayers. You know how I've been struggling at work."

Jim nodded and leaned back in his chair, folding his tanned arms.

"Well, one morning I asked God what I should be doing, and I believe he told me to write a book."

Jim's brow furrowed.

"I tried to write after work, but I was always too tired. I finally gave up and told God I couldn't do it." My cheeks flushed, and my palms began to sweat. This sounded crazy, even to me. Glancing to the ceiling with a silent prayer for help, I pressed on, staring at the table.

"God then told me to ask him for 'provision,' but I didn't know what he meant. I started asking for silly stuff, like a twenty-seven-hour day or the ability to stay up later than nine at night. Finally, I asked to be able to stay home."

PROLOGUE

Stealing a glance at Jim, I continued, "When that first letter came mentioning an inheritance, I told God if he *really* wanted me to stay home and write, I'd need it to be a year's salary." Leaning forward, looking into his eyes, I laid my hand on Jim's arm. "Hon, it's a little more than a year's salary. I need to quit."

Jim leaned back, pulling away from my touch. Tilting his head to one side, he silently stared at me. He finally looked away, shaking his head, "I guess you better quit, then."

"Really? You're okay with that?"

He exhaled a long, slow breath. "Yeah, but wait until it comes in. We don't know if it's real."

"Okay, that sounds fair." I couldn't stop grinning.

1
RAISED, NOT BORN

Riding to school with Mom in our old mustard-colored Corolla that first day of high school, I gazed out the window at Ho'okipa Beach Park as we whizzed by. Only a couple of surfers were out, as the waves were small and it was a Monday.

The dark blue ocean met the pale blue sky in a perfect line at horizon's edge. Hues of green revealed the shallow coral reef along the shoreline. Another beautiful day like so many I'd seen before.

How nice to swim in the cool morning ocean, I thought leaning my head against passenger's window, *instead of rushing down to dusty Kahului.*

Mom, eyes fixed on the road, hurried to make up for lost time. I don't know why I could never be ready when it was time to go. Most mornings I woke up late, rushed through breakfast, searched for something clean to wear, then pushed into Mom's bedroom (without knocking) to use her hairbrush.

There I'd find her, tidy in her nurse's uniform, kneeling beside her bed, eyes closed, hands clasped, quietly praying.

Prayer. Mom depended on it. Me, not so much. I thanked God before meals and asked for the things I needed every now and then.

"Sorry, Mom," I had apologized this morning.

"It's okay." She sighed, hoisting herself up and sitting on the edge of her bed. "Are you ready to go?"

"Just about."

Moments later, when she announced at the door, "I'm leaving," I was still scrambling to find my new folders, lunch money, purse, shoes . . . wait, had I brushed my teeth? Before I knew it, I'd made Mom late for work again.

Pulling into the student parking lot at Maui High School, Mom gave my hand a quick squeeze. "Have a nice day."

I looked at her, wanting to hold her tightly and cry and beg her to walk me to class, but, hearing a bell ring and seeing a few stragglers like myself running into campus, I chose to be cool. "Okay. See ya later!"

Coming from tiny Haiku School with its enrollment of 250 students in nine grades to Maui High with its 1,200 students in four proved both exciting and terrifying. My wallet held my shiny new student ID card, proclaiming me a Maui High School Saber, fooling me into thinking that I belonged.

Dreams of cheerleading, dating, and dressing up for romantic proms faded that first day as I pulled open the heavy blue door of my homeroom. I was late and all eyes were on me.

Sliding into the first available seat, I shrugged, murmuring a quick "sorry." The teacher, staring at me, reminded the class we were to be seated before the second bell rang. Feeling heat rise in my face, I stared at the floor until she finished the roll call. Unimportant announcements about the day's lunch menu and purchasing physical education uniforms followed.

Soon another bell rang, signifying the race to first period classes. Hundreds of students poured onto the concrete walkways, jostling for the fastest route down the corridor. "Sweet Jesus," I muttered, diving into the throng.

Hurrying down the gritty sidewalk onto the withered grass, I tried to nonchalantly glance at the map I held, wondering which ugly gray bunker was "B" building. *I should ask someone*, I thought, until I noticed the sophistication of the girls around me.

Feathered hair; flawless makeup; ankle-rolled, straight-leg Jordache jeans; and plastic "jelly" sandals rushed past me. Swallowing hard, I looked down at my faded off-brand bell-bottoms and Scott Hawaii slippers, quickly realizing I was on my own.

It wasn't bad enough being a mainland-born *haole* (Caucasian). If I'd at least been born on Maui, I'd be elevated to the status of "Born and Raised." But I was only raised. And, I was poor. And had a big nose. And freckles. Everywhere.

Finally finding my first class of the day—English—I slipped unnoticed into a seat against the wall near the back of the room. Being invisible came easy to me.

As the heat of the day grew, and anxiety over finding the right building and classroom waned, lunchtime arrived. Droves of hungry teens hustled into the overcrowded cafeteria. Standing alone in a long, noisy line, I inched toward the counter. A cute local guy with a dazzling smile and deep dimples walked over, asking, "Can cut?"

Well versed in the slang known as pidgin, I smiled back, nodding slightly. An older haole girl behind me cursed at Mr. Handsome, yelling, "Leave the freshman alone! She's still wet behind the ears!"

Not only did he cut in, he also brought several of his laughing friends. Feeling the anger of those behind me, I quickly paid my forty-five cents to the cashier, snatched the paper tray holding cold fries and a greasy burger, then escaped out the swinging double doors.

Seeing a few friends from Haiku sitting under a nearby tree, I joined them with a sigh.

"Hey," Trudy smiled.

"Hey."

From her dark Spanish eyes and stunning smile, to her easy laugh and innocence, Trudy was good. A quiet girl, she preferred reading to watching TV. She reflected her Christian faith with her modest wardrobe and clean language.

Trudy was the kind of girl I longed to be but wasn't. I knew I was supposed to be "different" as a Christian, but I was tired of being different. Growing up haole was hard enough. Adding virtue would make it impossible to fit in or be popular. Besides, I had Jesus in my heart, tucked away safe and sound, where I could find him if I needed him.

Trudy and I first met in Haiku School and attended the same church. We hiked, swam at the beach, and even went to youth group together a couple times. Trudy longed for a good Christian friend—one to share thoughts, secrets, and faith with—and thought she'd found that in me. But I was a chameleon. I bounced along, conforming to whoever was near.

One weekend, when Trudy slept over at my house, we sprawled across my old queen bed, reading. Suddenly, she stood, walked out, then returned without explanation. Assuming she'd gone to the bathroom, I didn't think much of it. But after her third escapade, I quietly followed her.

Hiding behind the open bedroom door, I peeked through the doorframe, watching as Trudy walked down the hallway and turned into the kitchen. Tiptoeing down the hall, I peered around the corner. There was Trudy, standing with an open jar of peanut butter in one hand and a spoon poised midair in the other.

"Aha! Caught you!" I squealed. Jumping nearly a foot off the ground, she stammered, "I'm so sorry! I know I should've asked. I . . . I love peanut butter and just couldn't resist . . ."

Doubled over, laughing, I told her, "It's fine! Please help yourself. Really, it's okay."

"Really?"

"Yes, of course. I just wondered where you kept going."

We giggled as she carried the jar down to my room. I'd never known anyone who so loved peanut butter! And, eating peanut butter all by itself? Hilarious!

Trudy's family lived far from town in Peahi, close to Twin Falls. Their home in the beautiful, rustic area sported no running water, electricity, or telephone. Even so, at my first sleepover I marveled at their stylish new home.

Her parents showed me their water tank and collection system, as well as their generator. It all seemed so normal. Normal until I went to the restroom, flushed, and sent her family into a mild panic.

"I think she flushed the toilet!" Trudy's younger brother exclaimed.

"She didn't know!" Trudy cried in my defense.

Trudy's dad, standing from the table where he'd been reading the newspaper, hurried out the front door.

"Uh, I'm sorry . . . ?" I began, confused.

Her mom grinned, explaining that their practice was to only flush when the contents weren't liquid.

"We have to fill the tank with a bucket from outside when we flush," she continued.

With only a small tank on the property for drinking water, the family collected rain for nonessential things like flushing the toilet.

Their lifestyle wasn't so much a matter of revolutionary self-sufficiency, though. It was simply because their property was so far off the main road that they would have to purchase the required telephone poles and water lines to tie into the grid. So, they chose to wait until more neighbors arrived to share the cost.

Without a TV, Trudy and I read and talked late into the dark night. I began to understand who she was, and why we were so different.

Back in school, Trudy and I didn't have many classes together but often saw each other at lunchtime. She was part of a group of "nerdy" friends that regularly gathered under a big tree in front of the cafeteria.

Kahului's heat kept students either in the overcrowded and noisy structure, or under the trees outside. Inside, the tables had established occupants. When not invited to join, I ate under the trees. My nerdy friends were my backup friends.

High school days passed slowly. Band was one of my better choices for classes, with its rowdy tunes for football games and marching routine for homecoming. Spring concerts were its boring downfall, though, requiring too much practice. Still, being in the band had perks as its classroom was one of only two air-conditioned buildings on campus. And it had clean bathrooms. So, I persevered.

Without encouragement at home to excel in academia, I only did enough schoolwork to stay off the teacher's radar. Reading was easy enough, and I quickly learned how to scan and find choice information for quizzes and tests. A quick glance in the morning over the previous night's assignment would usually garner an acceptable grade.

Once, wondering if I was smart, I tried an experiment. I actually *did* my homework in English class. For a whole week.

We'd been instructed to make vocabulary flash cards for our weekly tests and to accumulate all of the cards for a huge test at the end of the year. I'd never bothered with the flash cards, though. I felt my vocabulary was sufficient. Until the week of my experiment.

That particular week, I made my flash cards, read the required literature passage, and turned in an essay. On time. On Mondays, weekly scores from the prior week were posted on a bulletin board just inside the door for all to see.

Coming into class the Monday after my experimental week, the normal group of smart kids gathered around the bulletin board.

"Eileen, you're *third* in the class!" Arnold gasped. Smiling smugly, I strolled to my seat knowing that I *could* be smart if I wanted to be. But I didn't want to be. I reverted to my former apathetic self because smart kids were nerds.

My junior year, an assignment sparked another brief departure from apathy. Ms. Helt assigned a research paper on a "controversial subject" that would be presented to the class.

Abortion popped into my mind. Ms. Helt went around the room asking each of us what our topic would be. When I answered, her forehead puckered as she frowned.

"Are you sure you want to do that?" she asked.

"Yep."

No one else had received such a response from her. My topic, already seeming controversial, must be perfect. Not knowing much about abortion, except that my dad said it was wrong, I wondered what the big deal was.

Through my research, I soon discovered that a six-week-old fetus already had its own beating heart, and at nine weeks, earlobes. Fingers, fingernails, and even fingerprints were all a part of the marketed "blobs of tissue" that were easily disposed of should an unplanned pregnancy occur.

Outraged by my findings, I stood in front of the class presenting shocking pictures of aborted babies, perfectly formed mini humans, in trash cans. Concluding my presentation, I vehemently declared, "I am pro-life, and I would never, *ever*, have an abortion!"

I'd never felt so passionate about anything in my life. And I'd never stood up for something *I* believed in in front of a group of peers. It was a beautiful moment amidst the ugliness of truth.

An awkward silence followed until Ms. Helt asked if anyone had any questions. A few boys asked to see the photos, which I passed around the room. Though no one stood to throw roses or applaud, my mission was done. Or so I thought.

2

BECOMING HAOLE

Hurry!" my father's frustrated voice called out. Not knowing where to hurry to, I searched for Mom.

"Up!" I cried lifting my pudgy arms to her, but hers were filled with jackets, luggage, and papers. A stranger in uniform picked me up instead. Howling, I heard Mom's weary voice saying, "It's okay." Her taut face nodded as she patted my arm, then she turned, hustling my siblings down a steep, narrow staircase to a waiting van.

We were deplaning onto the tarmac of the Honolulu International Airport, dashing to catch the next awaiting flight.

The date was January 6, 1969, and I was two years old.

Delayed for several hours by inclement weather, our cross-continent flight had nearly stranded our family of six. The van whisked us away to the small interisland terminal for the last leg of our long journey. A missionary family from Eastern Canada, we quickly boarded the small plane and finally arrived at the only home I've ever known—Maui.

Life as a haole began.

Merriam-Webster defines *haole* (pronounced "how-lay") as:

> *Hawaii, sometimes disparaging + offensive*
> : one who is not descended from the aboriginal
> Polynesian inhabitants of Hawaii;
> *especially* : WHITE[1]

Moving to tropical Maui in the dead of winter, my parents gladly left all our winter apparel in the airport's bathroom upon arrival. They forsook their cold-wintered native Canada to serve as missionaries, first in Malaysia and Singapore from the late 1950s through the early '60s, and now, in Hawaii.

Diligently raising funds through speaking engagements, odd jobs, and puppet shows, Dad scraped together enough for the move and the required monthly support for this new mission. Using his charm and charisma to persuade airline staff, he even managed to bring several donated mattresses on the plane with us. Unfortunately, finding the mission not to be what he expected, Dad quit within months.

Without any intention of ever returning to the mainland, Dad quickly found work as a security guard at the Sheraton Beach Hotel. Though fearful of such a large payment, he and Mom signed a $125-per-month mortgage, buying our home on Ala Olu Place in rural Haiku. The old plantation camp house, built with used lumber, sat adjacent to a deep irrigation ditch for the pineapple fields nearby. After giving the house a thorough cleaning, Dad taped together odd pieces of used carpeting gleaned from a recent renovation at the Sheraton to cover the bare cement floors, and we moved in.

That first week there, a huge rainstorm hit. Unfortunately, with the street sloping toward our home, rushing runoff sloshed under our crooked front door, through the living room, across

---

1. *Merriam*-Webster, s.v. "haole," accessed March 26, 2018, https://www. merriam-webster.com/dictionary/haole.

the kitchen, and out the back door into the ditch. When the torrent subsided, we stood ankle deep in muddy carpet squares.

As soon as the sun came out, our neighbors arrived, unasked, with hoses in hand and rubber boots on their feet. They washed the mud from our now-bare concrete floors and pulled the donated mattresses outside to dry.

It wasn't quite the way Mom wanted to meet our new neighbors, but we did get to see their practical and helpful nature.

The following week, heavy rains fell overnight, and it happened again! I awoke that morning on a sopping mattress that I shared with my older sister, Kathleen. *She must have wet the bed*, I thought. *At least it wasn't me.*

When I splashed off the edge of the mattress, Dad picked me up, forcing my bare feet into my stiff, black Sunday shoes. "No! No shoes in house!" I protested in my three-year-old way.

"Just put them on!" he growled, starting me in a torrent of tears.

Gracious neighbors came over once more, repeating the same cleanup, and one of our heroes invited our family to dinner that evening. My parents gratefully accepted.

As mainland meat-and-potato people, we were unfamiliar with the staple starch of Hawaii—sticky, white rice.

Mom and Dad, unsure about the flavorless grain, asked for sugar and milk, in order to eat it as a rice pudding. Our shocked hosts provided what was asked and didn't laugh in front of the foolish haoles.

Eventually, my parents got the county to regrade the street. We never suffered floods like that again. And we learned to eat plain rice.

I would imagine that living in rural Haiku was much like living in any small town. Except that with an elevation of fewer than five hundred feet and bordering a tropical rain forest, we probably mowed our lawns a lot more often and saw more rainbows. And all of our neighbors sported a much darker tan than either my siblings or me. They also all seemed to be related to one another somehow.

Our neighbors were of Hawaiian, Japanese, Portuguese, Filipino, Puerto Rican, and Chinese descent. Many were the second and third generations born from immigrant workers on the sugar and pineapple plantations. The original immigrants had kept the race boundaries firm, but over time those lines began to fade and beautiful multiracial children were born.

Hawaiian children born with a mix of other nationalities were called *hapa*. If part Caucasian, they were *hapa-haole*. In my young mind, though, there were only two nationalities: local and haole.

Along with the evolution of the "local" nationality and the necessity of communication, language evolved from a base of Hawaiian and English to pidgin. Over time, this base was peppered with Japanese, Chinese, Portuguese, and Filipino words and phrases.

Entering the local Head Start Preschool at age four, I learned many new words. When finishing lunch, our teacher asked, "Are you *pau* (pow)?" Pau is Hawaiian for done or finished. We were also routinely asked if we needed to go *shi-shi* (she-she). This verbiage for using the restroom originated in the Japanese language.

We sat on our *okole* (oh-koh-lee), Hawaiian for one's bottom, and *hanabata* (all short vowels) often ran down our faces—*hana* being Japanese for nose, and *bata* as slang from the English word butter. No one wanted to be teased about *puka* (poo-kah) pants either. Puka is Hawaiian for hole. All adults were called either Auntie or Uncle as a sign of respect regardless of relation.

Back at home, Mom was a homemaker, selling Avon with me in tow, until I began kindergarten at Haiku School. Once I was in school, she started working full time, six days a week, as a nurse at the Maui Clinic. Without a formal nursing degree, she was trained on-site by the doctor she worked for.

After leaving the Sheraton, Dad worked various jobs selling everything from furniture to advertising, eventually opening his own massage business. Always looking for the latest trend, though, his business continued to evolve. He sold mini-trampolines, weight loss shakes, essence bottles, books, and even offered colon irrigation known as "colonics." Finally, he settled on selling Birkenstock shoes and medical uniforms. Unfortunately, his business basically supported his business.

While we weren't destitute, used clothing appeared for us in bags left at the front door. Even groceries arrived this way every now and then. We ate simple home-cooked meals and vacationed at the Waianapanapa State Park cabins in Hana, at the eastern end of Maui. Most everyone around us in Haiku lived just as simply as we did, so we were normal as far as I was concerned.

Being the youngest of four children, without a large extended family base or money to impress, I think I was doomed to obscurity from the get-go. Gordon, the oldest, was twelve years ahead of me, Eleanor was seven years my senior, and Kathleen was four years older.

Our age span was never planned, according to Mom, and she claimed she'd have had a dozen children had it been her choice. Dad seemed too busy to notice that we were around, unless we made him look good. Or, God forbid, made him look bad.

He enjoyed being the supreme leader, while Mom quietly went to work, came home, then cooked and cleaned for her lazy latchkey kids. Gordon, a quiet and relatively docile young man, never posed a threat to Dad's reign. But spirited Eleanor questioned authority and pushed the boundaries.

One evening, when I was around five years old, Dad called us all to dinner. For all the wrong things in our family, one thing we did right according to experts, was sharing dinner each evening. As we gathered around the table for this particular meal, waiting to pray and eat, Dad announced that, at the grand age of twelve, Eleanor was a young woman and now needed to dress for dinner.

When he ordered her to her room to change into a skirt and blouse while Kathleen and I sat in rumpled T-shirts and shorts, Eleanor's eyes widened as her mouth opened in protest. Pointing at us, she argued, "What about them?"

"What about them?" Dad challenged. "They're children. You are their example. Go. Get. Changed!"

We all turned to Mom, wondering what she thought, but she sat quietly staring at the table, trained to not interfere.

Eleanor humphed from the table, stormed to her room, and slammed the door. When she returned, nicely dressed, she curtsied grandly before flopping into her chair. I giggled, but Dad shook his head at me with eyes ablaze.

"That's how I expect you to dress for dinner from now on," he smirked, nodding at the rest of us victoriously. As he looked away, Eleanor frowned, sticking her tongue out at the back of his head. Jerking his face back toward her, Dad caught her wagging tongue. His hand smacked her across the face faster than an Olympic ping-pong paddle in a championship match.

Shocked, we all sat motionless for a moment until she ran from the table. I burst into tears.

I don't remember what happened after that. Maybe he apologized. Maybe he made her apologize. I do remember that Eleanor eventually stopped dressing up for dinner.

Dad's unpredictable outbursts often sent us scurrying to our rooms when his car pulled in the driveway at the end of the day. Though we were emphatically reminded to honor and obey our parents, it was tough when the rules kept changing with his moods. We never felt safe with Dad around.

Kathleen, a sensitive dreamer, escaped reality with flashlight in hand, reading late into the night under her blanket. Because we were the closest in age, we were rivals. In her mind, anyway. For fun, she made up elaborate tales of how everyone in our family was an alien. Everyone except me.

"See how Mom doesn't blink? That's because she's . . . an ALIEN!"

"Nooo . . . Mommmyyy!" I'd shriek, running to Mom for comfort.

Later, Kathleen would continue. "Mom really is an alien, you know."

"No, she said she's not!"

"Of course she said she's not. That's what aliens *have* to say."

"Waaahhh!"

One day, a new Christian horror film came out: *A Thief in the Night*. It portrayed an apocalyptic story of a young woman waking one morning to find that her husband, and millions all over the world, had been taken to be with Jesus in the rapture. But she'd been left behind. Kathleen enjoyed hiding from me so I'd think I was left behind.

Gordon was also a bit of a dreamer. He dreamed of blowing things up. Scraping the ends off the heads of matches, he made his own rockets, propelling our toys into the neighbor's pasture. Once he even made a rocket car which zoomed down the road until its plastic body melted into a red, gloppy mess.

Every now and then Gordon entertained us younger sisters with puppet shows or a scavenger hunt. Eleanor or Kathleen always won the hunts, since they could actually read the clues he'd left, but we laughed a lot, loving the small toys or pieces of candy at the end. Maybe he did this to alleviate the guilt he felt for melting our toys.

Me, I always yearned for attention. Not the "go change the channel on the TV" kind of attention, with which all youngest siblings of the 1970s were familiar, but the "you're really special" kind. I worked hard to make people like me, but I also had a temper and wasn't afraid to use it. Especially if I was hungry or tired.

After being told to change the channel too many times or to stand holding the antenna for better reception, I'd finally blow, yelling, "You're not the boss of me!" This became my catchphrase when asked to take out the trash, tidy up, or do just about anything I didn't want to do.

3

FITTING IN

As a young child I often played outside by myself in our small front yard in Haiku. An elderly Japanese neighbor, Matao, occasionally passed by on his way to the small store down the street. He lived alone, and wobbled as he walked, hanging on to nearby trees or posts for balance. Despite his difficulties, Matao carried a smile so big it nearly closed his eyes.

"Good morning!" my little voice bubbled, when I saw him on the street.

"Morning," he nodded back, waiting as I ran up to him.

"Look at the flowers I picked." I stood, holding out a handful of wilting dandelions for his inspection.

"Nice," he politely replied. As his body spasmed, knocking him off balance, he reached out a weathered hand and steadied himself against a nearby tree.

"Are you going to the store?" Though I knew the answer, I asked anyway. Matao seldom ventured further than the tiny Haiku Mart down the street.

"Yeah. I see you *bum-bye* (by and by)."

"Okay. Bye!"

Our friendship went on like this for years. Matao didn't mind this silly little curly-haired haole girl, and I enjoyed having a friend. While we seldom understood each other's words, we liked each other.

Mom often checked in on Matao, buying him Anacin for his aches and pains or offering rides to the store if it rained. On those rainy days, Matao brought pieces of old newspaper, painstakingly laying it down on the floor of the car to catch the mud on his shoes.

"Don't worry about it," Mom assured him. "The car's already old and dirty." But, ever the gentleman, he'd do it anyway.

Matao somehow learned that I loved chocolate milk and Cheetos. Back then, you could buy chocolate milk in single serving cans that didn't need refrigeration. Every now and then, on his way home from the store, he'd stop in our driveway, smiling and holding out a small sack containing these favorite treats.

Once, when Mom heard he was ill, she took him some soup. After he recovered, he went to the store and purchased a whole case of chocolate milk and a huge bag of Cheetos for me! Our family all wondered how he ever managed to carry them to our door.

Another Japanese man, Johnny, occasionally drove down our street in his blue Toyota truck to mow Matao's lawn and patch up his old home. Johnny was Matao's cousin, and we could see the family resemblance in their smiles.

As I got older, Mom and I talked about Matao after school one day. "Mom, I don't feel right calling Matao by his first name," I began. "Should I call him 'Uncle' or would it be better to call him 'Mr.' . . . hey, what is his last name?"

"His last name is Kusakabe. Koo-saw-kaw-bee," she drew out the syllables for me.

"Kusakabe? That's the funniest name I've ever heard!"

With my white skin and freckles, I stood out like a beacon light amongst my tanned classmates. Out on the playground one fine kindergarten day, I heard a new word: *haolecrap*. Wondering why an older local boy spat it at me, I decided to set the record straight. Standing tall, I proclaimed for all to hear, "I am not haolecrap. I am half American and half Canadian."

Suddenly, everything went silent. Children turned to stare. "What? What'd you say?" the boy glared down at me.

Thinking he must be hard of hearing, I repeated myself more loudly, "I am NOT haolecrap. I am half American and . . ."

As the gathering crowd erupted into laughter, poking each other and pointing at me, I realized my error. "Haole" and "crap" were two words.

"Again, haole!" they mocked, circling and pushing me. Mercifully, the bell rang.

In second grade, I was called behind a building one morning before school started. "Tori wants to see you," Heidi said. Feeling important that Tori wanted to play with me, even though she was only in kindergarten, I skipped over, stopping when I saw a crowd of older children.

"There she is," someone snarled.

Backing away, I bumped into a low-walled garden box. Unable to move any further, I sat down on its edge. Tori stood facing me, with her older siblings and cousins standing behind her chanting, "Hit her! Hit her!"

With tiny clenched fists, Tori thrust out her chest. "Stay away from my *bubba*!"

Looking back for approval, she was confused by the laughter of the crowd. Her sister pointed at my chin, "Hit her here."

23

Losing her nerve when she saw my tears, she glanced back and forth between her siblings and me, finally stepping back. The same sister, placing a reassuring arm around the little one, growled at me, "You better watch it!" Tori, rejuvenated, joined in with "Yeah! Leave my bubba alone!"

Not knowing what a bubba was, or what I'd done, I remained silent, focusing on the ground at my feet. The next morning, it happened again. But the third morning, when they called me behind the building, I didn't go. Terrified, I sat in front of the building, unable to move.

It ended then, as abruptly as it started.

Much later that I learned bubba meant "brother," though I never figured out what I'd done to incite the hostility. Ultimately, it didn't matter what I did or didn't do. I was a haole and bullying me was entertainment.

At the dinner table, I complained about being beaten up at school, though no one had actually hit me. The next day, Dad marched me into the principal's office, demanding something be done. As he berated the poor man and the entire system of education, I hung my head in shame.

After Dad left, the humiliated principal reprimanded my teacher, who in turn scolded my class. Whispers of "tattletale" were followed with "just wait till after school!"

Though nothing happened after school, the fear of future repercussions taught me to feign invisibility and made me very careful about what I shared at home.

As I learned the history of my island home, I began to understand the animosity I faced from my fellow students. The original missionaries to Hawaii, with good intentions toward the islands, brought Christianity and Western education. They also converted the oral Hawaiian language into a written language with the goal of making the Bible accessible for Hawaiians.

Unfortunately, they also imposed strict moral codes in an effort to change the culture. Hula was banned, and cumbersome Western styles of dress were imposed. The relaxed Hawaiian culture didn't bode well with the aggressive changes and superior attitudes of Caucasians.

While this sparked some of the negativity towards the haole, it was the missionaries' descendants that solidified the enmity. Referred to as, "the Big 5," these families became the wealthy and powerful plantation owners who recruited migrant labor from around the globe.

The original immigrants came from China, Japan, and Korea, and were joined by later arrivals from Portugal, Puerto Rico, and the Philippines. Low wages, a high cost of living, long hours, and segregation in camps were all part of the controlling immigration package. Mirroring slavery in the American South, *lunas* (foremen) even used whips to motivate these workers.

Generations later, when my family arrived, the undercurrents of distrust and anger toward haoles remained strong.

I never wanted to be white, so I spent hours in the sun trying to tan. With my impeccable pidgin skills, I could proudly pass for Portuguese, but my accompanying sailor's mouth made me feel guilty. Still, I wanted to fit in.

In fifth grade, I discovered a new interest: boys. My best friend, Lori, who was of Chinese and Filipino descent, didn't mind my race and was as crazy as me when it came to the opposite sex.

"Did you see *Happy Days* last night? Chachi is *so* cute! I wish I was Joanie," I giggled, rolling my eyes.

"Yeah, and he's going to be on *Love Boat*!" Lori squealed.

"No way! When? Oh, I can't wait!"

Chachi was acceptable to like. With his Italian heritage, he didn't look white. He looked hapa.

Lori and I shared a love of playing in the rain at recess time and passing notes during class. We volunteered for *cafe* duty as often as possible, and earned an extra carton of chocolate milk, a shortbread cookie, or a piece of peanut butter cake for our efforts. Of course, we would have worked in the cafeteria for nothing; getting out of class was payment enough.

As I got older, I knew if I wanted things, nice things, then I needed to work. In the spring of my eighth-grade year, I secured the illustrious job of developing a newspaper delivery route in Haiku. Traditionally, *The Maui News* was delivered a day after publication (a.k.a. late) with your mail.

But no more! With home delivery, you could get your newspaper the same day it was published.

Knocking on doors, I pitched this remarkable service to wary neighbors.

"Good afternoon," I called standing on a shaded front porch, peering through a screen door, where a local man sat watching TV in his living room. "Would you like *The Maui News* delivered to your home?"

"I already get 'um in da mail," he replied in pidgin.

"But I can get 'um to you the same day it's out," I countered in perfect pidgin.

"Nah, no need."

"K den. Tanks anyway." Shoulders slumped and head tilted down, I heaved a big sigh, turning to walk away.

"Wait. What's your name?"

"Eileen Millah (Miller)."

"Millah? Where you live?"

"Down the bottom of Kokomo Road." As was local custom, he showered me with questions about school, my parents, my siblings, and who I knew from his family. This normally revealed the hidden treasures of common friendships or the possibility of being related.

"Your father when help my uncle one time with one flat," he recalled, scratching his chin. That had garnered the sale. My Dad, for all his faults, also had a big heart for helping others. Whether my sales were from pity or friendship didn't really matter to me. It was all about the sale. You see, there were cash incentives for starting new customers.

While this first taste of free enterprise was sweet and exciting, the thrill quickly waned with the actual delivery work. I found that walking the uphill route on Kokomo Road with a heavy bag of papers on my shoulder wasn't much fun. Mercifully, delivery was only on Monday, Wednesday, and Friday afternoons.

At five cents a paper, along with the new-client incentives, my month-old route of nearly thirty papers amassed a whopping twenty-seven dollars! With the proceeds, I proudly purchased a brand-new dress for my eighth-grade banquet. Working was definitely the way to get what I wanted.

Shortly after I began the route, *The Maui News* expanded production to five days a week and added an early-morning Sunday edition. I quit before the changes took place. But I longed for money.

That summer, Dad found me a full-time job with a friend's business of gold-plating maile leaves (a native shrub). With the proceeds, I carefully purchased my own clothing, calculating the cost by the number of hours it took to earn each item.

Walking the mall, I found the latest straight-leg-jean styles revolting and expensive. It would take fifteen hours to buy a pair of those jeans! Surely no one would pay so much to look so ugly.

Opting for discounted clothing from a warehouse, I thought I was so smart.

4

REGRETS

E ileen, I made Junior Prom Court!" Trudy's ecstatic whisper cut through the haze of another boring school day. "Seriously?" I nearly dropped my lunch as I plopped next to her under the tree.

She nodded, laughing at my disbelief.

Trying to mask my jealousy, I congratulated her.

"Voting for the king and queen will take place next week." She jabbered on about picture taking and dance rehearsals, but I didn't hear her.

I'll never be anything.

Not popular enough for the court, I volunteered to help with decorations for the event. Our committee decided to embrace the Japanese tradition of Senbazuru, which is a folding of 1,001 paper cranes. The tradition began with a young Hiroshima survivor named Sadako Sasaki. When she fell ill with radiation sickness, her friends and family folded 1,001 paper cranes in an attempt to bring about her healing. Though she passed away, paper cranes became a symbol of hope.

The cranes were normally folded as a blessing for weddings, but our decoration committee thought it would be something different and fun for our prom. Of course, we didn't realize the amount of work involved. I carried those silly slips of paper everywhere, folding all through class, recess, and lunch periods. One day while folding a crane in social studies class, a young man asked me about them.

"It's for prom," I shyly replied. "Hopefully I'll get to go since I don't have a date yet."

After a brief pause, he said, "I'll take you if you want."

Now I didn't know this guy from Adam, but I was desperate. "Really? You don't have to." Part of me hoped he'd back out, as his eagerness didn't feel right.

"Sure! It'll be fun." He smiled.

And so I had a date to the prom.

After months of planning, buying my own dress, paying for both of our dinners (my date was unemployed), purchasing a traditional maile lei for him (with interwoven rosebuds, I might add), and getting my hair and makeup done, I found it just wasn't the magical evening I'd dreamed it would be.

My date turned out to be a desperate, lonely soul who didn't want me out of his sight all evening. And all the same cliques—the nerds, the cool kids, and the invisible, prevailed. The only difference was that we were overdressed.

Disappointed with the entire event and all the lies of how wonderful proms were, my thoughts nibbled at the corners of my mind about what other lies I believed. *What if life is just one big disappointment?*

As disappointed as I was, Trudy was thrilled. She and her prince, Kimo, performed the choreographed dances well, and thoroughly enjoyed being close to each other throughout the evening. They placed a very close second for the title of prom king and queen.

"I really like him," she told me the following week.

"I can tell," I smiled back.

"I don't know if he's a Christian, but he believes in God."

"And he's cute too," I winked.

Giggling, Trudy nodded.

As our senior year approached, Trudy blossomed. She cut off her straight, waist-length hair, revealing a cute wave in her new shoulder-length, layered hair. Contact lenses replaced brown-rimmed glasses, skirts switched to stylish jeans, and makeup highlighted her already beautiful complexion. Working at a local veterinarian clinic provided the financial means for her transformation and the purchase of her new wheels—a ten-year-old Toyota Celica. The faded-blue, two-door sports car ran well despite its age.

"Did you know that the insurance company charges more because it's a sports car?" she complained one day.

"You're kidding."

"No. It barely goes faster than forty-five miles per hour, and they charge me like I'm driving a Lamborghini!"

"Bummer! I guess you should have gotten a station wagon," I teased.

"Ugh. Yeah, maybe."

About the same time, I started working as a cashier at Woolworth's in the Maui Mall. My first week there, while training in the ladies department, I noticed a handsome stock boy. Dwain, with his tall and muscular frame, pushing a hand truck loaded with merchandise around the store, was a welcome distraction from counting underwear.

A former all-star football player, he had just graduated from rival Baldwin High and planned to move to Oahu for college in the fall. My first week there at Woolworth's was his last week. Too bad.

Still, I'd see him standing in an aisle, leaning on his hand truck, watching me work. I tried chatting about whatever popped into my head, but he would just smile and walk away. I couldn't keep his attention.

On his last day of work, he surprised me, asking if I'd like to go to a movie.

"I'd love to." I gave him a big smile. (He later confessed that he'd wanted to ask me out all week but couldn't get up his nerve. Since it was his last day, it didn't matter if I said no, as he'd never see me again.)

We dated until he left for school, and then continued our long-distance relationship through letters, phone calls, and his occasional long weekends at home on Maui. I'd sit in my high school classes, writing him long letters in my spiral-bound tablet, pretending to do my schoolwork.

When we were together, our relationship quickly turned physical, progressing further than my religion allowed. As he held me in his arms, the ache of wanting to fit in and to be cherished disappeared. Within months, I gave myself to him completely. The night it happened, I knew in my heart I would marry Dwain.

Years before, I'd read an article in a Christian magazine called *Campus Life*, where a girl asked if sex before marriage was okay since she and her boyfriend planned to marry. The counselor responded that since they would marry, the sexual sin wasn't as bad as not marrying.

At least that was my interpretation. Whether or not that was the verbiage used or the intent of the article is debatable. Once Dwain and I married, then our sin wouldn't be as bad. Right?

No longer a virgin, I walked my high school's campus wondering if those around me could tell. Did I walk differently? Act differently? Should I tell anyone? What was I supposed to do? But no one noticed. Life around me went on as if nothing had happened.

Trudy and Kimo had been selected as senior class representatives and were running for homecoming king and queen. Not your typical "football hero and head cheerleader" types, they were low-key and natural—regular friends that you knew would always be there for you no matter what.

Seeing Trudy walk towards me in the noisy cafeteria one Friday, I found it hard to look at her smiling face. What would she think of me if she knew about my sin? Would she still be my friend? I prayed she'd never find out.

As she slipped into the seat across from me on the long table, Trudy whispered mischievously, "Don't say anything, but I think we have a good chance of winning."

So completely absorbed in myself and my choices, I'd nearly forgotten that voting for homecoming king and queen was about to end.

"Ooh, do you have an inside scoop?" I leaned forward, matching her whisper, inwardly kicking myself.

"No, but one of the teachers that's monitoring the count mentioned that she saw a lot of votes for me and Kimo." Her shining eyes danced above her beaming smile.

"I'm so happy for you!" I reached across the table and squeezed her hand. "Don't forget us little people when you're queen, okay?"

"Okay." She laughed, turning to head out the door, preferring to eat lunch outside under the tree. I didn't want to eat out there anymore.

While voting ended that Friday, the results wouldn't be announced until Monday evening's bonfire and pep rally for the kickoff of homecoming week.

Anticipating next week's crazy dress-up schedule, lunchtime rallies, general fun, and mayhem, I started planning my attire. I loved dressing up! School pride day was easy with our school's blue and white colors. Class T-shirt day, another easy one. Switch day (always a favorite) meant a fake beard, some borrowed BVDs (briefs), Levis, and maybe a baseball cap.

I wanted this final homecoming to be one to remember. But inside I felt kind of numb. The distracting homecoming activities didn't ward off my guilty conscience over ruining my wedding night.

Don't think like that. It'll be fine. Lots of girls are doing it.

The next evening, Saturday, I walked with my flute in hand and the sound of Maui High's fight song, "Raunchy," playing in my head. "Go, Sabers, GO!" I yelled to the beat in unison with a group of band friends around me as we watched the team win the game.

Laughing and happy, we made our way down the bleachers and out the War Memorial Stadium gates with hundreds of other spectators.

Out in the parking lot, we stood talking, too pumped up to go home, wondering what to do next.

"Want to go to Burger King?" one friend asked.

"Nah, let's go to Minit Stop and have potato wedges," said another.

"Yeah, Minit Stop."

"Shoots!" I agreed in pidgin.

We all agreed this was where we'd meet. These were my "cool" friends, and I loved hanging out with them.

Trudy, wearing last year's homecoming T-shirt, walked over and stood next to me. "Hey there," she said, smiling.

"Hey."

Trudy was really nice, and innocent, and though we all loved her, she wasn't cool. Trudy was good, and for some reason, good didn't translate into cool.

Why did it matter that night? The others all quietly turned, slipping away until just Trudy and I remained.

"So, what's up? What are you doing now?" she asked.

Wanting to be cool, I shrugged and lied. "Oh, I don't know. I think I'll just go home. I have homework to do." My conscience pricked at me to invite her to Minit Stop, but I remained silent.

Trudy waited for a moment, as if reading my thoughts. Gazing at the ground, I didn't say anything further. Finally, she sighed. "Oh, okay. I guess I'll head home too. Bye."

She turned and walked away. Watching her retreating back, I felt a twinge of remorse and nearly called after her. But I didn't.

5

RAINY DAYS

As planned, I drove to Minit Stop, pulling into an empty spot not far from the front door. Seeing a few friends gathering, I joined them.

"What's up?" I called as I walked up the sidewalk.

"Nothing much. Want food?" someone asked, heading toward the snack shop's open door.

"Nah, I'm okay for now," I replied.

"Hey, there was an accident tonight!" Cherlyn exclaimed as she walked up. "Drunk driver crossed the center line."

Friends continued arriving, each adding whatever information they'd gathered passing the horrific accident.

"The road was closed in front of Star Market. Traffic's a mess!"

"Yeah, and I heard a Maui High student was killed!"

Gasps went through the growing crowd, and people pressed in closer to hear the gruesome news. As everyone talked at once, information came like rapid fire.

"I heard it was a girl in a Maui High homecoming shirt!" Arnold piped in.

"Yeah, and she was driving a blue Celica," said someone else.

What?

"Wait," I nearly shouted. "Trudy was wearing a home-coming shirt! And she drives an old blue Celica!" The hair on the back of my neck stood tall. The crowd went silent. Shaking, I saw the same shock and horror that I felt reflected on each face.

No, it simply couldn't be true. *No way.* Things like this didn't happen to real people. This couldn't happen here.

Denying what we had just deciphered, we quietly tried to reassure one another that it couldn't be true. I felt a hand on my shoulder. "Don't freak out, Eileen. We don't know that it's true." No longer interested in my friends, I walked to my car and drove home, numb.

During the long thirty-minute drive, I kept replaying Trudy walking up to me after the game and our conversation. She couldn't be dead! *I just saw her.* Surely it was some other student that I didn't know. There were lots of girls that wore their homecoming shirts. Surely there was more than one Celica driver at Maui High School.

Oh God, please . . .

At home, I found Dad sitting in the living room. "Hi, honey. How was your evening?"

Struggling, I started, "Something weird happened at Minit Stop after the game. When I got there, some friends were talking about an accident that happened. They said a girl who was wearing a homecoming shirt and driving a blue Celica was killed."

Dad stared at me intently.

"Dad, Trudy was wearing a homecoming shirt. And she drives a blue Celica." I gulped, trying to hold back the tears. "It couldn't be her, could it, Dad?"

"Don't worry about it." Eyes wide, he frowned and looked away. He mumbled something, but my racing mind couldn't understand. Exhausted, I retreated to my room, climbing into my old bed. The power of denial allowed me to sleep.

When I woke the next morning, Dad stood waiting outside my bedroom door. Placing his hands on my shoulders, he looked into my eyes. "It was Trudy."

"NOOO!"

He tried to hold me, but I fought his grip and continued screaming, "NO!"

This can't be real! Make it stop! Wake me up!

Mom came to me, but I pushed her away.

Pacing in the living room, I felt an unfamiliar coldness fill me.

Where do I go? What do I do? How could this have happened? Why didn't I invite her to Minit Stop? She wouldn't have been there at the accident site. She would still be alive. This is all my fault. Oh Lord, what do I do now? Oh Lord, oh Lord . . .

I was the worst friend *ever*. I didn't deserve Trudy's friendship. She trusted me. She wanted to be with me, and I sent her to her death. No one would love me if they knew the truth. It was unforgivable. I hated myself. Surely even God hated me now.

Dad followed me as I crumpled into a chair. Holding my head between my hands, I sobbed while he relayed the previous night's events.

"I called the police after you went to bed, asking if it was Trudy. The police said they hadn't notified the next of kin and that they couldn't release any information until that time." Dad continued, "When I asked them if they knew where the family lived, the officer said they were looking for the place. I offered to show them the home."

What? You were there when they told the family? That wasn't right. I couldn't process his words. All I knew was that Trudy was dead, and it was my fault.

My parents tried to console me with Bible passages about trusting in the Lord. It was the *last* thing I wanted to hear. Angry and unable to comprehend why God would do this, I pulled away, announcing, "I want Dwain."

Mom looked at Dad, shaking her head no, but Dad said, "Okay. I'll get him here."

Dwain arrived later that afternoon. Did Dad pay for his flight or just beg him to come? I didn't care. He was all I wanted. My expectations of comfort and help in finding some sort of meaning in all that was happening proved too tall an order for this eighteen-year-old young man. We wound up arguing instead. The stress only added more pain and guilt to my raw emotions.

On Monday, school seemed so stupid. Who cared about hyperbole or factoring polynomials? Book reports, grades, spelling lists—all just a big waste of time and energy.

Homecoming week began, with the homecoming king and queen voting results.

Kimo and Trudy had won.

But Trudy would never know.

In the gym, the daily pep rallies were fraught with bitter grief. No one had any answers or knew how to feel. Many of the old cliques evaporated. We weren't "nerds" or "cool" anymore, and it didn't matter if we lived in town or up-country.

Stripped of feeling young, safe, and invincible, we understood that it could have happened to any one of us.

Life suddenly became precious.

In the middle of one of these rallies, on "switch day" when boys dress as girls and vice versa, the school principal walked across the gymnasium floor. Pacing back and forth in front of the bleachers, scanning faces, he looked for me. Our local TV news team wanted interviews, and I was selected as "Trudy's best friend."

How could that be? I'm the worst friend ever! I am responsible for her death. Doesn't anyone understand?

Exiting the gym, I trudged over to the empty cafeteria where a reporter waited. On the way, I stopped in the girl's bathroom to quickly scrub off my penciled-in beard. Looking in the mirror, despising the face I saw, I turned away.

Three of us were called there for interviews: Leroy, the senior class homecoming representative; Kimo, homecoming king; and me—the best friend. We three rumpled students sat on one side of a long cafeteria table, quietly facing reporter Leslie Wilcox. She was seated, dressed in an immaculate two-piece suit. Speaking into a microphone, a cameraman filming our every move behind her, she began.

After asking simple questions of Leroy and Kimo, she turned to me asking, "Have you ever seen Trudy cry?"

What? What kind of stupid question is that?

I sat in stunned silence. My thoughts raced back to the only time I'd ever seen her cry. Heat rose to my face because I was the one who'd made her cry.

It was during our sophomore year in Mr. Yano's biology lab. We were seated in groups of four on tall metal stools, around shiny black tables, with a sink in the center. Trudy and I sat across from each other, with two other friends. Mr. Yano strolled around the classroom, holding his hands together behind his back.

"It is raining outside," he said, gazing out the window as he rocked on his heels. "Good day for a pop quiz. Take out your papers."

Groans erupted en masse.

"Did anyone read the lesson last night?" I whispered a bit too loudly.

"I remember your sister, Eleanor," Mr. Yano turned toward me. "She was a good student and did her homework. You are not like your sister."

Snickers murmured around the room.

"Thanks," I smirked. I was sunk.

Mr. Yano had us list numbers one through five on our papers. He methodically asked questions about the previous night's reading. My paper remained blank. Finally, I made up answers, hoping to bluff my way through. But he knew. I hadn't done much homework all semester. This was nothing new.

"Turn in your papers," he barked after a few minutes.

"Shoot. That was hard!" I grumbled.

"It wasn't too bad," Trudy innocently replied.

"Sheesh," I snapped at Trudy. "I guess if I had no life and read biology all the time it'd be easy for me too."

I thought I was so funny. But no one laughed.

As I saw the tears slip down Trudy's cheeks, I immediately felt as stupid as I looked. I'd made sweet, gentle Trudy cry. In class. In front of other people. Mortified, I glanced at our friends around the table. One shook her head, looking down at her notebook, while the other sat motionless just staring at me.

What was wrong with me?

"Oh Trudy, I'm so sorry! I didn't mean it, honestly." Digging a tissue out of my purse, I handed it to her. "I am so sorry. I can be such a jerk sometimes."

Looking up at me through her teary eyes, she'd said, "It's okay."

But it wasn't okay. And now this reporter wanted me to share that moment with the world? I glanced at her expectant stare, then down at the microphone she held in front of me, my gaze finally resting on the crack between the tables.

"No," I whispered.

Frowning, she turned back to Kimo and Leroy. I sat with heart pounding, wondering what was next. But she never asked me another question. Instead, she told her cameraman, "That's it. Let's go." He picked up his camera and she thanked us, swinging her legs around the bench to leave.

I couldn't let the interview end like that.

"Wait! Can I please say something else?" I begged, touching her arm. Leslie looked at me, and then turned to her cameraman.

"Get this," she ordered. Setting his camera back on his shoulder, he began rolling.

Nodding to me, Leslie said, "Go ahead."

"You were just in the pep rally a moment ago," I began. "You saw how our class pulled together on the floor of the gym to grieve. Trudy's death has stripped away all the divisions between us. Trudy was a beautiful person. She was a good person and didn't deserve to die. Death always seemed far away, but now we know it can happen at any time. Life can change in a moment. We appreciate one another now, and value life." I struggled to find something positive to say about what was happening.

"Thank you," she said shaking each of our hands before she left.

Our whole family gathered along with Dwain in our living room to watch the newscast that evening. An emotional wreck, I slept through most of it until Dwain shook me awake. Seeing our pep rally displayed on the screen, I vaguely heard my words describing Trudy in the background as the story closed.

The day of Trudy's funeral was a school day. It was a rainy day. A spectacular rainbow graced the sky as we drove down to the funeral home, and though it spoke of God's faithfulness through the ages, I felt no comfort and argued with God.

Why didn't you stop this, Lord? Why her? She's one that brought you so much joy. You're supposed to bless the good ones like her. Not let her be killed. It should have been someone that's not good . . . it should have been me.

Never before having seen a dead body, I peered into Trudy's open casket, not knowing what to expect. Her lifeless form was dressed in her white satin homecoming gown, her crown on her head, and a sash announcing "Our Queen" draped across her torso. It just didn't seem real.

Hundreds of mourners cut out of school to attend. Sobbing students filled every seat and stood shoulder to shoulder throughout Norman's Mortuary. The line to offer condolences stretched out the door and down the sidewalk out front.

Trudy's mom, dad, and little brother stood in the front of the mass of well-wishers, hour after hour, waiting for the line to dissipate. The funeral director finally stepped in, motioning the procession to stop, saying the service needed to begin.

The message given was one of hope in Jesus and of God's plan of redemption. It was a good word, but I felt nothing. I didn't deserve redemption. Printed in her program was a familiar verse:

> *Weeping may endure for a night,*
> *But joy comes in the morning.*
> —Psalm 30:5 (NKJV)

Once the service was done, hundreds of cars snaked in procession to the burial site. Black umbrellas dotted the memorial park in Haiku. Throngs of students surrounded the pretty white casket that waited to be placed into the hard soil. This was heartache beyond understanding. Trudy was gone.

6

HEARING GOD

Trudy was gone, but life went on. Dwain returned to Oahu, and school slowly returned to normal. Students resumed roles of being "nerds" or "cool" because we didn't know how to play any other way. Homework was issued and ignored. Work at Woolworth's went on as if nothing had happened.

But everything felt mechanical and as if I were watching myself play a joyless role.

Dwain completed his college semester that December and returned to Maui in time for my senior banquet, held at the Maui Lu Resort in Kihei. While there we ate, danced, took our formal picture, and then snuck away before the banquet's end to be alone in a rented room.

The room, with its ample supply of alcohol and junk food, had been rented with a group of friends for a night of youthful fun.

Early the next morning, after saying goodbye to our tired and somewhat hungover friends, Dwain and I stepped outside into the brilliant sunshine of a new day.

I heard the words *You're pregnant.*

Turning to the left, where the voice seemed to come from, I saw no one, though I really didn't expect to. Instinctively, I knew God had spoken, but I dismissed the unfamiliar voice.

And yet, as much as I didn't want to be pregnant at seventeen or have a child right away, somehow it felt true. My spirit accepted it, while my flesh doubted my sanity. *How could this be happening? I knew* it was real. But I never told a soul. Not even Dwain.

A few days later, using the restroom at work, I noticed some spotting. Thinking my period was starting, I felt mildly disappointed. The voice I heard must not have been God after all. Good thing I'd kept it to myself.

Dwain and I, being both young and selfish, found that we really had nothing in common beyond physical attraction. As that attraction diminished, much of our time was filled with arguing. Nothing was off limits. Clothing, where to eat, which friends we spent time with, what was on TV, and even whether or not to go to church.

Tired of the constant tension, we finally broke off our relationship. I wanted nothing more to do with him.

In school, pretending all was well, I went on to win the title of Miss Saber Spirit in the spring. The week of rallies, class competitions, and basketball games culminated in the crowning ceremony midgame on Friday night. It should have been the highlight of my senior year.

Instead, I anxiously waited and wondered when my period would start. How long had it been? Two months? Three? And that spotting at work—was it a period? It hadn't even lasted a day.

Fumbling along, I went to school, then to work, slept whenever I could (often in class), drove home, collapsed, got up the next morning, and did it all over again. Still no period.

I knew I was pregnant. My clothes weren't fitting right anymore. My breasts hurt. What was I going to do?

In my social studies class, we were offered a voluntary stress test. Secretly, I checked off several factors that seemed to fit, like:

- Death of someone close to you

- Unexpected pregnancy (though not yet confirmed)

- Breakup of a relationship or a divorce

I felt a strange pride that I hit so many of these highest-scoring stressors and still held it all together. At least I pretended to hold it together. Mostly I squished all my guilt and fear deep down so I didn't have to think about it.

After weeks of restless nights, I broke down. It happened on a Sunday afternoon in my parents' bedroom. After a morning at church and a light lunch, my sister Eleanor, very pregnant with her third child, rested on the bed. Her husband, Gary, sat on a chair near the window, reading. I slumped on the edge of the bed near Eleanor.

"Hey, girl," she smiled.

"Hey."

"Everything all right?"

"Not really. Can I share something with you both?"

"Sure." Eleanor rolled on her side, leaning her head on her elbow.

"I think I'm pregnant."

Time stood still as my words sank in.

Eleanor sat up and wrapped her arms around me, holding me tight. Gary came up from behind, putting a hand on my shoulder. They didn't chastise me. They didn't hate me. They let me sob.

"You need to be seen by a doctor," Eleanor calmly stated, "and get it confirmed."

A plan formulated around me. Gary said something, and Eleanor responded, but all I felt was relief that I wasn't hated. Despite the tremendous shame of my sin, I wasn't hated.

That night I slept soundly for the first time in a very long time.

Eleanor made arrangements for me to see her gynecologist the following week. After months of denial, I finally considered the possibility of pregnancy. What would I do? I couldn't have an abortion. I'd seen the pictures. It was wrong.

But, being young and single, I couldn't care for a baby either. Should I give it up for adoption? What about college? And what about the coming summer band trip to Japan? Four years of fund-raising and two years of Japanese classes would be wasted if I didn't go.

Maybe I'm not pregnant.

When the appointment date arrived, Eleanor met me at the doctor's office, gave me a hug, and told me that, no matter what, it would be okay. Wanda, a friend from church, was the nurse who began the exam. "Why are you here today?" she asked.

"I think I'm pregnant," I whispered, staring at my hands. Wanda reached over, squeezing my knee. "It'll be okay."

Feeling my heart pounding, I nodded, not believing her.

Wanda took my blood pressure and weight and then gave me a sealed plastic cup for a urine sample. When that was done, she sat me in an exam room while she ran a pregnancy test. When the doctor came in, he touched my swollen belly. "Well, you're pregnant . . ."

Pregnant.

"Your parents don't have to know; we can schedule a date . . ."

Cocking my head to one side, I thought his words made no sense. Once I understood, I exploded, "I don't want to have an abortion!"

"Well, you'll have to tell your parents then!" he retorted.

No kidding.

"And just what do you intend to do with the baby?" he scowled.

"I'll give it up for adoption."

"If you love the baby enough to have it, you won't be able to give it up."

It sounded like a challenge.

When I came out, Gary was there in his postal uniform, waiting with Eleanor. "Well?"

I nodded yes, and the tears started. Wanda shuffled all of us into her office, giving us a few moments of privacy. Once we gathered ourselves, we thanked her and left.

Stepping outside the front door, I was surprised to see Mom walking up the sidewalk. She knew my period was late and had hurried over after work to meet us. "What did the doctor say?" she asked.

"He gave me some vitamins," I mumbled without looking at her. Instantly, she figured out what was happening but said nothing. Taking a step back, she said, "I'll go get Dad, and see you at home." She turned, leaving as quickly as she had arrived.

Home. The last place I wanted to be.

"Let's go for a drive," Gary suggested. Gary drove as I cried in the front passenger seat of their sedan, Eleanor behind me. He pulled into the shaded parking lot of Kepaniwai Gardens in Iao Valley and rolled down the windows.

Switching off the car, Gary turned to me. "What are your plans for the baby?"

"I'll give it up for adoption."

After a moment's pause, Gary responded, "Then give the baby to us."

A gasp erupted from the back seat.

"Don't let this baby out of the family." Gary's stare bore holes into my adoption resolve. Thinking this was *my* baby, I'd never considered it as a member of the family.

Gary spoke of his own birth out of wedlock, reminiscing happy times of growing up with his mother, aunt, and cousins. Though it was hard, Gary's life proved it was not only doable, but that a babe born out of wedlock could have a wonderful, meaningful life.

"Why don't you want to keep the baby?" he quietly asked.

"Keep it?" I pondered aloud. I hadn't even considered it. "I . . . don't think I'm capable. I'm still in school."

"You'll be done with high school by the time the baby arrives. You could raise this child." Gary spoke with such authority that I nearly believed him. Staring out the window at the trees above, I wondered about being a mother. *A mother.*

"You wouldn't be alone. Eleanor and I will help, and so will the rest of the family. I believe in you. With God's help, you can do this."

It was the first time I'd ever heard anyone say that they believed in me or that they thought I could succeed. Warmth slowly filled me.

"You really think so?"

"I know so."

I leaned back against the headrest, closing my eyes. A *baby!* My heart, now that of a mother, burst with joy! *This was the right thing to do.*

"Okay." I slowly voiced the momentous decision. A small smile pulled the corners of my mouth. "I can do this."

Yes! I want this baby! MY baby!

Gary's smile mirrored mine. We hugged, cried, and prayed for my baby and for the strength to face Mom and Dad.

"Oh, thank goodness!" Eleanor grinned, wiping her eyes. "I didn't want to raise *two* babies only four months apart!"

"They'd be like twins!" I laughed. "Hey, our children will grow up together."

They drove me back to my car, and then followed me home to deliver the news to Mom and Dad. I envisioned Dad flying into a rage, having a massive heart attack, and dying on the spot. Mom would hate me for the rest of my life for killing Dad.

When I pulled into our driveway, I waited for Gary and Eleanor to park. As we slowly walked down the sidewalk together, I wondered what to say. But I didn't need to wonder.

Opening the front door, with Gary and Eleanor behind me, I saw Mom and Dad sitting at the dining table, waiting. My brother, Gordon, lay on the floor watching TV, still in his dirty work clothes.

"You're pregnant?" Dad questioned, with an eerie calmness about him.

I nodded, looking at the floor. Gordon jumped up, snapping off the TV. Eyes wide, he turned, facing me. "What?!"

"Your mother told me she thought you were pregnant as we drove home." Speechless, I couldn't read Dad. "Well," he continued, "I told your mother that you can still live here and that we'll support you in any way we can."

"Thanks," I muttered, staring at Dad's cold eyes.

Still live here? They considered kicking me out?

Gary and Eleanor stood silently behind me, watching the exchange. Tension filled the warm evening air, like the moments between thunder and lightning.

Gary finally broke the awkward silence with "Well, we better go." Eleanor gave me a quick hug and hurried out the door. Gary, putting both hands on my shoulders, said, "You'll be okay." My tear-filled eyes locked with his, silently begging him to stay.

But he didn't stay. He followed Eleanor out to their car and gave a quick wave as he got in. I stood there in the doorway, watching them drive away. Closing it gently after they left, I turned to face my parents.

7

NO OTHER WAY

Once they were gone, Dad released his fury. Eyes bulging, sweat beading on his red face, he spat his words. "How dare you. How DARE you do this to me! How could you shut me out of your life?" Punctuating each phrase with the shaking finger he jabbed at me, he ended with a shrill "How could you?!"

Fists clenched, I replied in kind. "Shut you out? What are you taking about? As if you care! You are always gone! You never have time for me or anyone else!"

We glared at each other, sharing a long moment of pure hatred. I turned away.

There would be no hugs here. No words of support. No prayers. Yes, I had blown it, but I didn't need this.

Mom stepped in, trying to turn the boil down to a simmer. Putting a hand on Dad's shoulder, she soothed, "Tommy—"

"Quiet!" he snapped, shrugging off her touch. Scowling at me once more, he stormed away. A door slammed.

Mom sighed, dragging herself into the kitchen. She wouldn't even look at me. Dishes rattled as she prepared a dinner no one wanted.

Gordon had been watching everything with tear-brimmed eyes and now looked like a beaten puppy. Turning away, he went into his room, quietly closing the door behind him.

Shaking and alone, I didn't know what to do. Oh God, if this was support, I'd hate to see opposition.

For three days after our initial exchange, Dad stomped through the house muttering curses under his breath. If I caught his gaze, he'd fix his fiery eyes with such a venomous glare it made my skin crawl. Always frowning, he slammed his bedroom door, the bathroom door, and every cabinet door he touched, as if I might have missed that fact that I was under his wrath.

But he never spoke directly to me.

Fine. I don't need you!

I hadn't asked for Dad's input in years. I couldn't remember him ever asking about my classes or grades. Once, when cutting out of school with a carload of friends, I drove right up to Dad's office to ask him for gas money. Opening his wallet in front of them, he handed me a twenty-dollar bill, saying I needed a day off.

"Your dad is so cool!" they had gushed. I wasn't so sure.

My clothing never got a second glance either. I'd been working, buying what I wanted, doing what I wanted, and going where I wanted for years.

But now I'd gone too far.

Mom, always cordial, dared not cross the battle line Dad had drawn. Coming home from work, she edged through the house, cleaning and cooking, and then quietly retreated to her room. Poor Gordon followed suit, with the exception of cooking and cleaning. He just hid in his room.

I stayed away from home as much as possible, avoiding Dad at all costs. School and work kept me away most evenings, and when I was home, I'd hide too.

Late one evening I sat alone in the living room, doing homework, thinking Dad had gone to bed. After days of silence, he startled me, walking in with a big announcement. "I'll allow you to keep the baby," he stated grandly. Nodding and dramatically clasping his hands, he continued, "Mom has been struggling with thoughts of raising another baby and wants you to give it up for adoption. But I told her you could keep it," he lied. (I found out later that Mom was the one insistent on keeping the baby and supporting me at home. He would have thrown me out.)

What? Of course I'm keeping this baby!

Blinking several times, I furrowed my brow. Knowing it was time to end the battle, I bit my lip, responding with a respectful, "Okay. Thanks."

Dad then sat next to me, pulling me onto his knee like a little child. Though repulsed, I obediently tolerated the action.

"When your mother told me you were pregnant, she also said, 'God will teach us things through this that we can learn no other way.' " His voice quavered. "She is a wise woman."

"Yes, she is," I whispered. We stiffly hugged and I stood. The tsunami of wrath turned into a cold stream of acceptance.

A week later, I mentioned to Dad that I didn't know how to tell Dwain about the baby. He quickly looked away. "He already knows."

"You told him?" Incredulous, I could only stare as the revelation sunk in.

My heart thundered in my chest. *How dare you!*

"When did you tell him? Exactly what did you say?" My voice raised a pitch with each phrase.

"He just knows, okay?" he snarled, turned, and walked away.

I stormed into the kitchen. "Mom, did you know about Dad telling Dwain?"

Mom slowly turned from the sink filled with suds and dirty dishes. "Yes, I knew. You need to talk to Dad about it." She wiped her hands on a dish towel hanging from the oven's handle, and her sad eyes found my angry ones. She rehung the towel and walked to her bedroom. I heard papers shuffling.

Walking back to the living room, I glared at Dad. Mom came in, handing me several envelopes addressed to me but already opened. They were letters from a lawyer.

"What are these? Why are they opened?" Pulling one of the letters out of its envelope, I shook it at Dad.

Dad's face turned white. He quickly deflected my anger with a lie, "Dwain is denying that the baby is his."

I felt as if I'd been punched.

The letters fell to the floor.

"How can that be?" I whispered. "He knows it's his baby."

Mind racing, I tried to understand why he would deny paternity. Dwain and I broke up in early January, and it was now the end of March. He'd followed me on the lone date I'd had before I knew I was pregnant. Surely he didn't think that guy was the father!

But it didn't really matter. Dwain knew. He knew and he'd never called.

Torn between the loneliness of wanting Dwain to hold me and the anger of my life being over, I waited for him to contact me. It was so unfair that he could go on and do whatever he wanted while I couldn't. I was stuck with a million decisions to make and the shame of my growing belly while his life seemed unchanged.

Did I want him in my life? In the baby's life? Maybe it was best to just stay away and raise the baby by myself. All alone. *Why didn't he call?*

Weeks later, I finally drove to the gas station where Dwain worked, hoping to speak with him. I didn't tell my parents, as I knew they wouldn't approve the visit.

Pulling into a parking stall next to the station, I saw Dwain for the first time since I'd learned about the baby. The awkwardness of being pregnant by this man, wanting to strangle him and wanting his arms around me at the same time left me a mute mess. I wanted to make it right, but how?

Sitting in my car, I saw his head jerk when he caught my eye. He spoke to a coworker, and then made his way over to me. I thought I'd be sick. My heartbeat pounded in my ears as I rolled down my window.

"Hey," he started.

"Hey."

"How you feeling?" he asked.

"Fat."

We spoke for all of ten minutes. He confessed his initial doubts about being the baby's father, as we'd broken up a couple months before he learned of my pregnancy. But, deep down, he said he knew the baby was his. He'd even started putting money aside to help out.

Dwain's father had received the fateful call from my dad, and in turn questioned Dwain about our relationship. Dwain went on to say he'd wanted to call me but thought it would be safer to stay away.

"Safer to stay away? What are you talking about?"

What my Dad had failed to mention when he told me that Dwain knew of my pregnancy was that in his initial outrage, he'd called Dwain's father threatening to shoot Dwain. Twice. *Twice! Good Lord.*

And the mysterious lawyer's letters? Dwain knew nothing about them. Dad had probably contacted a lawyer in my name. I never saw the letters again and never heard anything more about them.

When I got home that evening, I spoke with Mom about seeing Dwain. She told Dad about it, and Dad forbade me from ever seeing him again. With his threat of being thrown out of the house still in mind, I obliged. For a time, anyway.

As my pregnancy progressed, I started cutting out of school at lunchtime, attending only the classes I needed for graduation. Walking the hallways alone, I overheard conversations of college pursuits and the upcoming band trip to Japan.

Outside of school, walking the mall amplified my loneliness. Watching pregnant couples smiling and holding hands, and babies in strollers pushed by pairs of parents, nearly killed me. Then, on the other end of the spectrum, I spied groups of teens hanging out, shopping, and laughing like I used to do.

But I no longer fit in my jeans or in society. Ugly pants with a stretchy panel in front, huge billowing blouses, and muu muus (Hawaiian-print, loose, waistless dresses), were all that fit now.

By the time graduation rolled around, I was ready to be done with school. Many classmates, planning to go away to mainland colleges, wondered about GPAs, majors, and scholarships. Planning my nursery, I wondered about cloth diapers, pacifiers, and breastfeeding. With nothing in common, I lost touch with my peers.

Work at Woolworth's continued along with school, with me squeezing in enough hours every week to maintain my desperately needed medical coverage. After graduation, full-time hours helped me save a bit for future needs.

At home, Dad tried to fix my life by suggesting I marry one of his older bachelor friends.

Unbelievable!

Hadn't he made things hard enough? The palpable tension between Dad and I made for a miserable home. Poor Mom.

In early October, after a long and difficult twelve-hour labor, little Brandon entered the world. Having suffered through the labor with me, Mom wept when she saw him. Whether it was from relief or exhaustion, I wasn't sure. Brandon's stretched, cone-shaped head looked like the Muppet Bert from Sesame Street; he even sported a pokey tuft of hair at the cone's peak. At first glance, I feared brain damage. Brandon, wide-eyed, looking all around, didn't cry like babies always did in the movies.

"Why isn't he crying?" I asked.

"Do you want me to make him cry?" the doctor chuckled.

"No, not if you don't have to." Confused, I turned to Mom. As the nurses whisked him off to the nursery, Mom patted my shoulder. "He's fine."

Many visitors came to see Brandon. Though he was born out of wedlock, all the shame faded away with one look at his sweet face. Classmates came, church people came, and Dwain came.

Two days later I rode home with Mom, and the world looked so beautiful and bright! Gazing at the little bundle in the car seat beside me, I marveled at being a mother.

This baby was my son.

Pride and happiness filled my soul. Did I have a plan? No. Any idea of how hard it would be? Nope. I was just happy. At eighteen, I didn't have enough life experience to understand my new responsibilities. What a blessing.

8

ENDINGS AND BEGINNINGS

The first few days with a newborn are pure survival, plain and simple. And, wanting to do the best I could for Brandon, I chose to breastfeed. It was the hardest, most wonderful thing I'd ever done in my short life.

Having to stop, sit still, and hold my son several times a day and throughout the night forged a bond like no other. It was also the cheapest way to feed him.

After about a week of breastfeeding induced sleep deprivation, I looked at the clock in my room: 6:30. Gazing outside through bleary eyes, I couldn't tell if it was 6:30 a.m. or 6:30 p.m. I also didn't know what day of the week it was or when I had last brushed my teeth.

Mom was a lifesaving help, even though she worked full time. As soon as she came home, she'd scoop Brandon up and let me nap. Then, after an hour or so, she'd hand him back, head to the kitchen, and make dinner. Mom walked Brandon up and down the hall those nights I couldn't soothe him, and she loved him as fiercely as I did.

Our church offered financial assistance so I could be home, asking only for a list of expenses. Wonderful people in the church donated money for diapers, clothing, and even babysitting should I need a break.

As grateful as I was, I hated accepting charity. I'd always taken care of myself, and this was *my* mess. I would straighten it up myself. With my mom's help, of course.

When Brandon was four months old, I went back to work at Woolworth's part time, setting my work schedule to coincide with every moment Mom was off work. I never even consulted her. Mom now had no time to go shopping, see a doctor, or do anything besides work and babysit. Though she never complained, she seldom smiled.

Since I had an income, I thanked the church for their help and asked them to stop. Now my son needed a father.

I went out on a single date with a fellow from church, but the whole evening, all I felt was guilt and shame.

First love's power, that intense spiritual bond of sexual intimacy created by God to seal a couple's union in marriage, held me. Even though Dwain and I were apart, I couldn't date anyone else. We needed to raise our son together.

Hoping to earn God's approval and maybe balance the scales of the universe back in my favor, I vowed to make it work with Dwain. The old adage of making my bed and now lying in it never seemed truer.

Dwain and I began dating again and quickly decided to marry. In January 1986, we started our new life together as a married couple. Married with a rambunctious toddler, that is. We'd forgotten how difficult our relationship had been *before* Brandon. I'll never know why we thought his addition would smooth away all our former problems.

"And they lived happily ever after" didn't happen. After a tumultuous six months, I left Dwain. By December of the same year, we were divorced.

Washed up at the ripe old age of twenty, I couldn't even buy beer yet to drown my sorrows. My life's score card: Pregnant teen, check. Unwed mother, check. Uneducated, check. And now the granddaddy of them all: divorcée.

Initially, I moved back home with my parents, but the ever-increasing tension between Dad and me made everyone at home miserable. Through a friend, Dad found a little rental cottage I could afford about ten minutes from home. Perfect. Being on my own for the first time in my adult life was a wonderful, scary, and lonely time.

I read and reread biblical passages regarding divorce and remarriage. Convinced that I would cause a man to commit adultery if he married me, it seemed my only options were remaining single or reconciling with Dwain. Reconciliation was out, though. We weren't compatible, and he'd moved on.

Was I destined to be alone? Was that God's plan of punishment after divorce? I didn't know what to do, but I knew I was lonely. And I wanted an in-house daddy for Brandon.

In our church I watched other people divorce and remarry, so I asked my pastor about it. He spoke with me at length, asking my thoughts on the subject. I told him what I'd read, and my conclusion that I had to reconcile with Dwain or stay single.

While he agreed with the Bible, he asked, "Do you think Dwain will remarry?"

"I think that's where he's headed."

"Do you think God wants you to pray for Dwain's second marriage to fail so you can reconcile?"

"Of course not. I wouldn't want anyone to go through that," I truthfully replied.

"Then I think it's reasonable to say that once he remarries, your commitment is done. You'll be free to remarry."

Right or wrong, that sounded like good reasoning to me.

When a kind haole guy from church asked me out, I gratefully accepted. We dated for nearly a year, but our relationship didn't progress quickly enough for my liking. We held hands and kissed good night, but what did that mean? Was he my boyfriend or were we just friends?

Seeking a more defined relationship, one that ultimately ended with "and they lived happily ever after," I finally asked a loaded question while driving home one night after a date. "What are we?"

Staring off into the distance for a few moments, he finally stated, "We're nothing more than we are right now. Is that okay?"

While I wanted to shout, "What the heck does that mean?" I instead answered, "Yeah."

Glancing at me, he smiled, giving my hand a quick squeeze. Disappointed, I couldn't smile back.

A few weeks later, we sat on his couch, flipping channels on the TV. Venturing back into unwelcome territory, I asked if there was a future for us.

He stiffened. "I don't know." Turning off the TV, he walked over to the huge picture window fronting his house. Staring at the twinkling lights of Kahului in the distance, he pushed his hands into his pockets.

Seeing the discomfort my question posed, I still pushed on. "I need to know we're heading for marriage."

"I can't give you an answer tonight. I'm thinking about it, but there's a lot more involved than just you and I."

"True," I conceded, thinking of Brandon. "Can you just assure me that there is a future for us? If not, then I want to know that it's okay to date others."

Taking in a deep breath, he slowly exhaled. "Then maybe we should just be friends."

Ugh! Not that!

Silence stretched between us.

"Okay, if that's what you think is best." Picking up my purse, I headed for the door before the tears fell.

The next morning, I stood in Mom and Dad's kitchen, sadly relaying the previous night's decision. My father shook his head, grumbling, "He's a fine man! Why'd you push him? You should be grateful he'd even date you!"

Grateful he'd even date you. His cutting words confirmed my worthlessness.

"Thanks a lot, Dad," I snapped back, swiping away the tears.

Dad sighed.

Then he asked an odd question, "Who else are you interested in?"

Who else am I interested in? I am just coming off a painful breakup! I'm not interested in dating anyone, thank you very much.

Rolling my eyes, I looked to Mom for help. After watching our exchange in silence, she simply shrugged and turned away.

Truth be told, there was a man I'd secretly admired for some time. Even while dating my last suitor, I was curious about the quiet and handsome Japanese man at church. He was local, and I still held the deeply ingrained desire to marry a local guy and have local children. Besides, Brandon was half Japanese. Wouldn't it make more sense to marry someone of the same heritage?

This mystery man and I shared mutual friends, but we had never said more than a quick, "Hello" or "How're you doing?" to each other. At church, I looked for his car and tried to park nearby, hoping he'd notice me. Every now and then, I'd hang around the back of the church after the sermon while he duplicated copies of the message on cassette tapes.

He never noticed me, though. It was a silly crush. One I hadn't shared with anyone.

Dad watched me as if reading my thoughts. Wanting me married and settled, he waited for an answer. Stupidly, I volunteered, "I've always admired Jim Kusakabe, but he's way out of my league. He's older and would never take a second look at someone like me." Dad nodded, turned, and walked away.

Huh, that was weird.

Three days later, Dad called me. "Are you going to be in tonight?"

I briefly thought about the day and replied, "No, I think I'm going to Bible study. Why?"

"You need to be home tonight. Skip Bible study." Then, he hung up.

"What? Why?" I spoke into the dead phone line. *Oh no! What's he done now?* Redialing Dad's office number, I waited as the phone rang and rang. He wouldn't answer.

I quickly dialed Mom's work number. "Good afternoon, Doctor—"

"Dad called and said I have to be home tonight," I interrupted. "What's going on?"

Mom cautiously replied, "Well, Dad may have gone to see Jim, and he may be calling you tonight."

What?

Taking in a sharp breath, I tried to keep my voice even. "And just what might he have said when he spoke with Jim?"

A few moments of silence ensued before Mom carefully responded. "You know Dad means well. He told Jim that you like him and that even though there is a big age difference, he has our blessing to ask you out."

Oh no.

"Please tell me you're joking, Mom."

She sighed, repeating, "He means well. I think it'll be fine." She sounded as if she were trying to convince herself of the same thing.

I hung up, flopped on the couch, and looked at the ceiling.

"Oh Lord, what's going on? I don't want this." Humiliated and angry, I thought, *I should just go to the Bible study and show Dad that I don't need his help!*

Still, what if Jim did call? But why would anyone in their right mind want to call after being told so bluntly to do so?

A little after 7:00 that evening the phone rang. Hands sweating, nerves on edge, I picked up the receiver. "Hello?"

"Hi. This is Jim from church. I was wondering if you might like to go to dinner on Friday night."

My heart fluttered. "That sounds good. What time would you like me to be ready?"

"Oh, how about 6:00?"

"I can do that. Thank you."

The conversation lasted only moments, but I had my first date lined up with Jim Kusakabe! I wanted to kill and hug Dad all at the same time.

Jim arrived to pick me up in his old Toyota Tercel, looking handsome in slacks, a reverse print aloha shirt, and leather shoes. We drove to a restaurant called Mark Edison's in Iao Valley for dinner. When the waiter arrived, Jim ordered a beer and asked if I would like a glass of wine.

"Wait, are you old enough?" he teased.

"Yes, I'm over twenty-one. Barely, but I am legal, thank you very much."

Our conversation evolved around the food we ate and our jobs. He was easy to talk to and had a quick laugh. When dinner was done, he asked if I would like to drive over to Kihei for a walk along the beachfront.

"Sounds good," I replied, not wanting the evening to end. After a quick ten-minute drive, Jim parked the car along the roadway, and we strolled down the sidewalk, parallel to the crashing ocean.

"How are your feet doing?" he asked, nodding toward my high heels.

"Oh, they're fine. These are actually pretty comfortable."

"Well, my feet are sore. I don't wear these shoes very often, and I'd like to go home and get some slippers."

"That's fine by me." I laughed, feeling happy to see where he lived.

We pulled up a steep driveway and parked in front of an old green shack. It was mostly green, anyway. The faded and peeling paint was flecked with spots of bare wood. A new gray roof looked to be in good shape, but the rest of the place did not. Warped stairs led up to an old white, windowless door with a ceramic doorknob.

Jim smiled as he told me the story of getting this shack near the beach. It was an old plantation home owned by the C. Brewer Corporation, and when he began working for them, they offered it to him rent free. Though the property it sat on had since been sold to a developer, Jim was allowed to stay.

"I still don't have to pay rent," he bragged. "But I had to agree to move out once the new owner gets his permits to build. When I first moved in, the roof was caved in, and the place was in bad shape," he commented.

Was in bad shape?

"I put on a new roof and replaced some termite-eaten wood here and there. But with no rent and being so close to the beach, I can't complain."

We walked up the creaky front steps and went into the living room. A single, naked bulb hung from the center of the ceiling, illuminating the room. An old, green-striped couch fit in well with the faded walls and dirty windows. Looking around at his surfboards, kayak, and diving gear, I saw how the location suited him well.

"No rent is amazing! Hard to put a lot of work into the place, though, as you know it will eventually be torn down," I observed. He grinned at me, seeming glad that its condition didn't send me running.

Jim slid off his shoes and sighed. "Ahhh, that's better." Quickly putting on his slippers, he led me back out to the car. Driving back to my cottage where Mom and Dad babysat three-year-old Brandon for me, Jim said, "I had a good time."

"Me too."

"Maybe we can do this again sometime . . . ?"

"I'd like that." I smiled at him.

Dad hurried to the car as we parked. "So how'd it go?"

We both grinned, saying, "fine" and "good" simultaneously as we climbed out.

Jim shook Dad's hand and waved goodbye before getting back into his car to drive home. Dad eyed me curiously. "Do you have another date lined up yet?"

"No, not yet," I rolled my twinkling eyes. "But he said he had a good time and asked if I'd like to do it again."

Satisfied with my response, Dad gloated. "My job's done. Time to go home."

Many years later, I learned more about Dad's "dating intervention." At the time, Jim was working for C. Brewer & Co., Ltd., as a supervisor in their pineapple operation. From my understanding, their interaction went something like this:

Dad visited Jim, arriving with a bribe of coffee and donuts, quickly getting to the point. "I'm here for my daughter, Eileen. Do you know who she is?"

"Yes, I've seen her at church."

"Well, she likes you, and I think you should ask her out."

Jim sat, listening quietly as Dad pushed his agenda. "She's young, but you have my permission to date her. In fact, I give you my blessing. I'll make sure she's home on Wednesday night so you can call her. Here's her number."

"Uh, okay," Jim stammered taking the slip of paper Dad held out to him.

"You will call her, won't you?" Dad persisted.

"Yes, I'll do that," Jim agreed.

Dad would have made an amazing used car salesman.

9

COMMERCIAL BREAKS

After that first date, Jim and I dated pretty much every weekend. We went for beach walks and bike rides. We took Brandon fishing off the pier near Jim's shack in Maalaea and we ate. A lot. Jim, an amazing cook, made delicious picnics of anything from Cornish game hens to Portuguese sausage and eggs.

Sadly, his cooking skill had developed because his mom passed away from cancer at the early age of forty-five. Jim, thirteen at the time and the older of the family's two children, was told by his father, "If you like eat, cook!"

Jim's father, Johnny, whose parents had emigrated from Japan to work in the sugar plantation, had also lost his mother at a young age. Without a woman's influence in either home, there seemed a loss of understanding of the gentler sex. (More than the average man, anyway.)

As an adult, Johnny continued in the plantation life, becoming an expert welder and supervisor for Maui Pineapple Company. He valued hard work and self-sufficiency, and expected the same from Jim and his sister, Claire. To that end, for Christmas one year, he bought the squabbling siblings boxing gloves to settle their own disputes.

When I was a child, it was this same Johnny that I had seen, in his blue Toyota truck, driving up my street to help his cousin, Matao.

I'd never known a man like Jim. He carried a self-assured confidence that made me feel safe. Of course, his thick black hair, nicely trimmed mustache, and broad shoulders didn't hurt my opinion of him in any way either.

A month after our first date, for my twenty-second birthday, he gave me a card featuring sausages, dressed in green alpine caps, with drawn-on mouths, singing. On the inside, it offered birthday wishes from the Vienna Sausage Boys' Choir. Loving his sense of humor, I was smitten.

He wasn't impulsive in any way, especially when it came to spending his hard-earned money. Thinking he should buy something for aerobic exercise, he went to the library (this was before Google), researched reviews, warranty, and lifespan of differing equipment, finally settling on a NordicTrack Pro Skier.

He was smart. I could seldom tell him anything he didn't already know. And he killed the dictionary game! With friends, we'd open the dictionary searching for an unfamiliar, ridiculous-sounding word, and secretly write out made-up definitions on index cards. Points were earned with votes for the best-sounding fake definitions and also for identifying the correct definition. Jim won every time.

Intrigued by this solid, upright, and dry-witted man, I found myself falling for him fast and hard. Opposites really do attract.

For nearly a year, Jim never once tried to hold my hand or kiss me good night. My friends joked, "He must be gay."

I didn't know what to make of it. While he seemed to enjoy my company, he wasn't affectionate.

I'd tried romantic music, touching his arm when we walked together, even leaning close when we sat beside each other. But he never responded. I wasn't even sure he noticed I was a woman. How would I ever make Jim marry me? And, even though Jim and Brandon both liked the same outdoor activities, Jim seemed unsure of what to do with my energetic young boy. How would that work out?

One Saturday, after a long morning at the beach, the three of us drove back to Jim's place with a large pizza in the back beside a hungry four-year-old Brandon. Smelling the wonderful scent of warm bread and melting cheese, he began to cry.

"Is it okay if I give him a piece while you drive?" I asked Jim.

"Can't he just wait until we get there?"

Turning to Brandon, I soothed, "We're almost there, honey. Think you can wait just a little longer?" Reaching behind me, I rubbed his sweaty leg, but the crying turned to wailing. Taking off my seat belt, I crawled beside him, quickly pulling a slice from the box.

"Here you go, have a bite."

Jim shook his head, saying, "You shouldn't spoil him like that. We're not that far from home."

"He needs to eat," I retorted.

"Well, don't make a mess."

Make a mess? Good grief! This poor kid is starving, and you're worried about your ten-year-old vinyl seats?

"Okay," I sighed. Brandon's wailing turned to whimpers between the chewing and swallowing, and then he fell asleep.

Later that summer, some friends of ours planned a weekend camping trip in the Polipoli State Park, where they'd secured the only cabin. Though they invited both Jim and me, I reluctantly declined. I had an interview for a new job with the postal service that Saturday.

Jim, wanting me to come along, offered to drive to the cabin Friday evening after work, back for the interview Saturday morning, and then return to the campsite after the interview.

"That's a lot of driving," I remarked.

"Not a big deal. I don't know what else to do up there anyway."

By this time, I had learned that Jim was a bit of a recluse.

"Okay, if you're sure about it, I'll see if my folks can watch Brandon. Thanks!"

"No problem," he smiled.

Friday evening, he drove the long, dusty road to the cabin, and Saturday morning he drove me back home as promised, in plenty of time to clean up for the interview. The interview itself went smoothly, concluding with "You'll hear from us soon."

Jim returned to pick me up late Saturday afternoon. As we made the trek back to camp, we talked about my interview and the possibility of this new job.

"It would be so good!" I gushed. "Not only is the pay better but so are the benefits. I wouldn't have to work nights, and I'd get federal holidays off." It was fun contemplating the future with Jim.

Feeling happy and excited, I told him that I liked him. A lot.

In fact, I plainly stated, "I think I might be falling in love with you. But I don't know if that's a good thing or not."

Jim sucked in his breath and didn't answer.

This is the part where you're supposed to say, "I love you, too." I waited, but hope swirled away like the dust plumes behind us.

"I enjoy being with you," he slowly began, "but our age difference is pretty big." He was fourteen years my senior.

Uh oh. Here it comes.

"I don't know what to say," he grimaced.

"Sorry, I shouldn't have even brought it up," I mumbled. *Why did I say anything? Stupid, stupid, stupid!*

"No, it's good to talk about," he assured me. "I'm flattered."

We rode in silence the rest of the way. I practically leapt from the car when we arrived. At dinner, I couldn't look at Jim. Roasting marshmallows around the fire pit, I ignored him. I even considered trying to find a different ride home. But I couldn't. Not after he'd been so nice to drive me around so much.

The next day, I slunk into his car feeling doomed. There was no avoiding it now. I had to face up to my pushiness again. "Had a good time?" he spoke gently and offered a weak smile.

"Great," I lied as he started the car.

Winding down the dusty road, he started, "About yesterday—"

"I'm sorry, I never should have said anything," I interrupted.

"No, it was a nice thing to say. I like your companionship."

My face felt hot as I stared out the window, silent.

"I think we're headed somewhere," he explained. "Honestly, I really struggle with change. I just don't want to rush."

No kidding.

Wanting to climb into the glove compartment, I silently berated myself the rest of the way home.

We continued to date, but never spoke further about my profession of love. I vowed not to push Jim, as that had killed my last relationship, but waiting wasn't in my DNA. It was yet another vow that I'd break.

Later that week, I received word that I was hired at the Makawao Post Office as a part-time flexible clerk. Though it was classed as part time, I basically would be working a full-time schedule stretched over a six-day week. But I didn't care. I was thrilled. Goodbye Woolworth's!

That fall, Jim held my hand. Once. It happened in the parking lot of the Maui County Fair as we walked back to his car. In an unusually joyful mood, he crossed in front of me, snatching up my hand as he passed. Surprised, I said nothing for fear of losing the moment. He never looked at me, but I saw a smile on his face from the corner of my eye. Sadly, he dropped my hand when he opened the car door. It must have lasted all of five minutes.

The following year, as my birthday approached, we were out driving when Jim turned to me and asked what I would like for my big day.

"What I'd really like is a promise ring." The words shot out of my mouth faster than Ralphie's "I want an official Red Ryder, carbine-action, two-hundred-shot range model air rifle!" in *A Christmas Story*.

Oh no . . . where'd that come from?

Slumping down into my seat, I knew I would have had better luck asking Santa.

After a short pause, he replied, "What's a promise ring? I've never heard of it before."

Swallowing to steady my voice, I answered casually, "It's a small ring with a diamond that signifies a promise that a relationship is going somewhere."

"Oh."

It was a big risk to ask for such a thing, but I wanted progress. Brandon was getting older, I wasn't getting any younger, and I wanted a man at home.

After a longer pause, Jim finally asked, "Where would you get one?"

Did I hear correctly?

Trying to hide my smile, I said, "Oh, any jewelry store should carry them."

"You'll have to help me find one."

"Okay."

A few days later, we stood at the jewelry counter in Sears. A nice couple from our church, Steve and Debbie, spotted us. Coming over, they looked at my ring finger. "Anything we should know about?"

"No, no, we're just looking at promise rings," Jim quickly said, holding up both hands.

"Oh, that's exciting," Debbie remarked, smiling.

"Why waste time? Go for it!" Steve poked Jim in the ribs.

I cringed knowing I was lucky even to have gotten this far with Jim. To my surprise, he just laughed with them.

We picked out a ring with a Hawaiian motif. The thin, gold band was intricately carved with patterns and leaves, and the tiny diamond winked in the showroom lighting. It was beautiful. Unfortunately, it needed to be ordered and wouldn't be in for a week.

After Jim picked it up, he presented it to me in his driveway. As I put it on, he kissed me for the first time. On the cheek.

A year later, Jim and I sat on his old couch, watching TV as we had done countless evenings before. Most weekends, we picnicked at the beach for dinner, or he would cook at his place.

Now that we'd been dating for so long, we seldom went out to eat. Jim didn't like driving the half hour to pick me up at my place, either. So I'd bring Brandon down to his place, we'd eat, watch TV, or rent a video, then I'd pack Brandon up and go home.

Occasionally we went to weddings or parties together, but that was about the extent of our dating experience. He was comfortable. Too comfortable. I was restless. Needless to say, it was time for a change.

His shack was so run-down that termites swarmed indoors on warm, still nights. On one of those nights, we lured the little pests away by turning off the naked bulb in the living room and turning on the bulb in the kitchen. Mercifully, they preferred the bulb's light over the TV's glare.

It was in this romantic setting that I waited for a commercial break, and brought up the subject of our relationship. "Is this really leading somewhere?"

Jim sighed. He *hated* serious talks, especially ones on feelings, thoughts, goals, or—God forbid—marriage.

"Because it's been over two years now," I pressed. "I think that's long enough to know if we're compatible."

The show he was watching came back on. I had to wait. Again. *Humph.*

When the next commercial break came on, Jim spoke before I could nag him further.

"Fine," he grumbled. "We can get married."

"Really?"

He peered at me, then rolled his eyes. "Yes. Really."

Huh. Well, this wasn't the engagement I had envisioned. No dreamy Zales or Ben Bridge ads here. *Wait, did I just force him to marry me?*

"You'll have to come with me to get the ring, because I don't want to get something you don't like," he ordered.

"Oh. Okay." Funny, I didn't feel very excited.

The show came back on.

10

GROWING AGAIN

We married the following April, a little over three years after our first date. Jim was thirty-eight and I was twenty-four when we said our vows. Climbing into our Rolls Royce getaway car (rented as a wedding gift from our pastor), we laughed at our personalized "Just Married" sign. Jim's best man had crossed out "Just" and wrote "Finally" above it. I couldn't have agreed more!

A new life began with a new last name, one that I'd once claimed was the funniest name I'd ever heard: Kusakabe.

Returning home from our honeymoon, we started life together as a family. Jim gave up his free shack on the beach and moved into the cottage Brandon and I shared. He also started a new job with the C. Brewer family as an industrial chemicals salesman. It was a huge change, but one that held a more secure future for his new family.

Jim's father graciously gave us permission to build a new house behind his home in Makawao. The project, started in January, was about halfway done when we married in April. Poor Jim worked all day at his regular job, then joined his dad and our contractor to work on the house until dusk.

Brandon, energetic and excited to play with his new dad, looked forward to Jim's arrival at the end of each day. But Jim was exhausted. Most nights he'd walk in, eat dinner, and fall asleep on the couch in front of the TV without much interaction with either of us.

"It's okay, Brandon," I whispered one evening. "Dad will be able to play more once the house is done."

Adding to the stress was my own struggle with endometriosis—a disorder where tissue that normally lines the inside of the uterus is found on the outside. With each monthly cycle it spread, causing pain and adhesions that could lead to infertility.

The birth control I used slowed its progress by lightening my cycles, but ongoing inflammation was a problem. My doctor decided to temporarily switch me to steroids in an attempt to reduce it, assuring me that their use would create a near-menopausal state, preventing any pregnancy.

While Jim and I had never broached the idea of having more children, it really didn't matter. I welcomed the idea of adding to our family and was sure that Jim would too.

Life was moving along nicely. Our new home was finally finished in July, and we moved right in. Unpacking our dishes and placing them neatly in our new kitchen cabinets, I smiled, thinking about how blessed we were. New marriage, new home, new life. I would be happy forever.

But Jim was still the same Jim as when we dated. He went to work, cooked dinner, then sat on the couch with a plate of food and watched TV. Marriage hadn't produced any miraculous romantic changes. He didn't arrive at the door with bouquets of flowers or boxes of chocolates for his new bride. There were no romantic candlelit dinners. And there were lots of dishes.

Brandon, now six, bounced around his new dad, often blocking the TV, as he tried to get Jim to wrestle, play tag, or go outside and play ball. But Jim was Jim. If he went outside, it was to water his plants or mow the lawn.

My expectations of magical, memorable, Kodak family moments weren't happening. Worse, my suggestions for improvement (a.k.a. whining) seemed to push Jim more into himself. He'd normally respond with a shrug, throw his tired "It's how I am" at me, then retreat alone out to the yard or into his greenhouse.

Frustrated after arguing with him one evening, I flew to our bedroom in a rage. Kicking the door open, I heard a miserable crunch as the doorstop broke a nickel-sized hole through the wood laminate. Horrified, I heard my Dad's singsong voice in my head:

There was a little girl,
And she had a little curl
Right in the middle of her forehead.
When she was good
She was very, very good,
And when she was bad she was horrid.

—Henry Wadsworth Longfellow[2]

I hated that poem. As embarrassed as Dad's recitations had always made me feel, I knew it was true. I did have a short fuse, especially if I were tired or hungry. And now, as an adult, I feared perpetuating the same manipulative anger I'd been raised with.

Confessing it to the Lord, I begged for patience. Of course, I assumed patience could be bestowed as a gift. I never imagined it had to be earned or that it might cost me something.

---

2. Henry Wadsworth Longfellow, "There Was a Little Girl," *The World's Best Poetry*, ed. Bliss Carman , vol. 1, *Of Home: Of Friendship* (Philadelphia: John D. Morris & Co., 1904), http://www.bartleby. com/360/1/120.html.

Apologizing to Jim, I showed him the hole in the door. He didn't shout or appear angry. He just shook his head and wondered aloud how to fix it. His quiet Japanese upbringing, with discipline, honor, and self-control genetically embedded, always kept his temperament even.

Sports became the answer for Brandon's boundless energy. He began playing all year round—soccer, basketball, and baseball—with one season ending as the next season began. He was a gifted athlete, and I enjoyed being Team Mom as often as I could.

After several months of learning how to live together, I began experiencing tenderness in my chest. Recognizing the feeling from my pregnancy with Brandon, I checked the calendar. Sure enough, I was late for my cycle. Sharing my excitement with Jim when he came home from work, his head fell, and he began rubbing his temples with his thumbs.

"I thought the doctor said you wouldn't get pregnant," he said quietly.

"Yeah, that's what I thought too." Certain that he was just tired, I ignored his displeasure. "Still, I should probably pick up a pregnancy test."

Jim groaned and walked away.

A few days later, as the sky lightened for a new day, I sat in the bathroom with the pregnancy test in hand. Two little yellow beads in a small glass tube would soon let me know if my wish was coming true. Completing the test, hoping for one of the beads to turn blue, I waited. Hints of blue began to appear immediately. Smiling, I set the tube down next to the sink.

Crawling back into bed with Jim, I decided it would be best to wait the recommended time, just to be sure.

"Well, what did it say?" Jim asked.

"It said to wait 5 minutes."

Jim said nothing more. We lay together in silence. Standing up, I walked back to the bathroom to see. Jim jumped off the bed, following at my heels. Sure enough, the little bead was as blue as the ocean!

"Well?" Jim demanded.

"I'm pregnant!" I squealed trying to hug him.

"Oh no!" he cried, pushing past me and collapsing on the bed.

"No, no, no!" he repeated, shaking his head. "This is just too much! I can't handle it!"

Frozen where I stood, I stared at this man whom I'd pledged to love forever. Stretched out on his back with his palms pressed against his eyes, tears rolled into his hair from the corners of his eyes.

"You're not happy?"

"We just got married! I'm still trying to figure out how to be a father to Brandon. Add a new job, new house, moving—*twice*—it's too much!"

Goosebumps ran down my spine. "So you don't want the baby?"

"Yes, of course I want the baby," he quickly reassured me. "I am just overwhelmed by all this change. It feels like everything is out of control."

"So, I shouldn't be happy?" I wanted to be happy . . . together.

Jim sighed. "Yes, be happy."

He sat up, rubbed his eyes and looked at the closet. "I have to get ready for work."

"Should I not tell anyone?"

"Do what you want."

I began to cry.

Putting a hand on each of my shoulders, he looked into my tear-filled eyes. "Sorry, it's just a huge shock. Just give me time to get used to the idea."

"Okay, I can do that." I forced a smile.

Brandon, on the other hand, was thrilled! Already in the second grade at Makawao Elementary, he couldn't wait to be a big brother like his friends. Brandon was sure the baby would be a boy.

"But you'd love the baby if it was a girl, right?"

Brandon cocked his head to one side, scrunching his lips together. "Yeah, I guess so." Then he grinned, saying, "But it'll be a boy," and bounded away.

About four months into my pregnancy, my dad found out that his cancer was no longer in remission. Back when Dad had turned sixty, he'd marveled at his long life, exclaiming, "No one in my family even lived to be fifty, and I've had an extra ten years!"

Earlier that same year, he'd been diagnosed with lymphoma, and he expected to die. Enduring a single, painful cycle of chemotherapy, he quit treatment. "Everything hurts," he'd complained. "My joints hurt, my teeth hurt. It even hurts to pass gas!"

Miraculously, though, that one treatment had garnered him remission. His doctors warned him that he still needed to complete several more cycles, but he refused, stating, "I'd rather die."

Now, just over a year later, the cancer had returned. With no desire for Western medicine, Dad sought homeopathic means of combating the lymphoma through a two-week program taught in Mexico. The regimen included a strict vegan diet, boatloads of juiced vegetables, and coffee enemas. To his credit, he fought the way he lived his life—on his own terms.

As the cancer spread, swelling his abdomen, the tumor forced his belly button outward, producing a hideous wound.

One afternoon, lying in his bed, Dad asked me to come and sit with him.

Placing his cool, wrinkled hands on my growing abdomen, he closed his eyes and started praying, asking God's blessing on this babe. Tears streamed down my face as I realized he knew he'd never see my child this side of heaven.

Dad's half-brother, Walter, called from the mainland announcing that he too had just been diagnosed with lymphoma. He wanted to know what Dad had done and what he needed to do. Dad simply replied, "Put your affairs in order. You're going to die."

Dad passed away in May of 1992, ten days after he turned sixty-two. Walter passed away six months after Dad, at the age of fifty-four. Dad's revelation of no one in his family living to age fifty unnerved us four siblings, but we never spoke of it. Denial is a powerful weapon.

After Dad's funeral, my pregnancy progressed uneventfully. Though Jim wasn't happy, he did go to Lamaze classes with me. When my due date passed by one day, then two, three, four . . . it felt like the baby wasn't ever going to be born. Finally, our new son made his grand appearance ten days late.

As soon as Jim saw his baby, tears again fell. But these tears were full of joy. Jim couldn't stop smiling! All the months of frustration and anxiety melted away in an instant.

"You did good, Eileen," he complimented me, rubbing my shoulders as we gazed at our new son.

The next afternoon, we brought Owen home. Family and friends showered us with meals, gifts, flowers, and hugs. Jim took off work for a couple of weeks to settle in and get to know our new son. Brandon was thrilled.

"I told you, Mom!" he proudly proclaimed.

"Yes, you were the only one that knew he was a boy," I winked back.

It didn't take long to see that Owen was very different than Brandon. He cried a lot and hated all that Brandon had loved as a baby, like bath time, car rides, the bouncy chair, and (my favorite) the windup swing. Brandon would have lived in that swing had he not needed diaper changes.

Even though I'd only had one child prior to Owen, I could tell something wasn't right. He carried a huge umbilical hernia, and the way he struggled to hold up his head made him seem more of a blob than a developing baby.

At a well-baby checkup, I tried to articulate my concerns to his pediatrician, but he told me that all new mothers felt inadequate.

Inadequate? Humph!

When it was time for me to return to work, Jim and I discussed Owen's poor development, and I told him I was worried about leaving Owen with a sitter. Eventually, we made the difficult decision for me to quit my job and be a homemaker. While I was ecstatic about not having to rush out the door every morning, the lack of income was terrifying.

At two months of age, Owen developed a double testicular hernia requiring surgical repair on Oahu. His pediatrician said not to worry as this was pretty common in children.

What we had yet to learn was that there was nothing common about our new son.

11

HOMESCHOOLING:
AN OXYMORON?

When Owen was ten months old, we attended a Lamaze class reunion. Watching Owen next to his peers, my heart sank. While most babies were sitting, scooting, and getting up on all fours, Owen lay relaxed on his back. He never made any effort to move.

What am I doing wrong?

Another mother came alongside me, quietly mentioning a local nonprofit organization with a program for developmentally delayed infants. Her manner was so gentle and nonjudgmental, that I decided to explore the program.

When I took Owen in for his consultation, they offered us speech, physical, and occupational therapies, all covered through our insurance and private donors. Starting weekly visits with their therapists, I learned exercises and strategies to help Owen and felt sure they would "fix" him.

The "tactile sensitivity" label given him helped us understand some of Owen's challenges. Bathing, bright lights, grass, sand, loud voices, even certain fabrics made him shriek. Often.

We were told that his overly sensitive nerve endings and immature neurological pathways meant that everything he experienced felt like pain to him. The goal was to desensitize him so he could function more normally.

Despite the challenges, Jim and I were very happy with our new addition. We were so happy that we made another one. When we told Brandon about another new baby, he said, "It'll be a girl. You need a girl this time."

Though everyone's opinion of my growing frame was that I was having another boy, Brandon insisted it was a girl. Once again, he was right! Elyse joined the family one sunny April morning. A contented baby, she slept through the night at just six weeks old.

Thank you, Jesus.

Elyse grew up watching Owen's therapy sessions, often joining in and learning right alongside him. They developed a special bond working together.

As Owen neared the program's graduation age of three, testing was recommended to help us with his preschool placement.

During one of these evaluations, his physical therapist discussed the tactile sensitivity, referring to it as a sign of retardation.

"Retardation? That can't be," I challenged. "He can walk and speak. He can learn. I thought he was only delayed." Granted, he needed custom insoles to walk, and he needed me to interpret much of what he said. But retardation? That word had never before been associated with Owen.

"He is doing well," Owen's therapist carefully affirmed. "But he's still well behind his peers."

Her associate, a woman I'd never seen before, silently observed our exchange. Looking at me through narrowed eyes, she suddenly blurted, "What drugs did you use while you were pregnant?"

"Drugs?" I looked from one woman to the other. "I only took vitamins. What do you mean?"

"Marijuana? Cocaine?" she fired off.

"Nothing like that. *Ever.* I didn't even drink caffeine while I was pregnant." Confused by her tone, my face flushed.

"What about alcohol? How many drinks did you have every day?"

"None whatsoever." I glared back. *Does she think his delay is my fault?*

"I see." Her pursed lips and tilted head betrayed her thoughts.

Our session over, I quickly scooped Owen up, put him in our double stroller with Elyse, and hurried away.

At home that evening, I relayed the conversation to Jim. Listening intently, he offered no solution. I had always assumed Owen's delay was a bump in the road that we'd overcome and move on. Now I didn't know what to think.

Was this my fault? I'd taken some extra vitamin C when I was pregnant. And what about those steroids I took that were supposed to keep me from getting pregnant? Did they do something unfathomable to Owen?

The next morning, I knelt in prayer at my office chair. *God, I don't know what to do. You've made Owen as he is, and I don't know how to fix him. I don't want him to struggle. Help me, God.* Mom's words to Dad came to mind, "We will learn things through this that we can learn no other way."

What am I to learn Lord?

"Patience." The silent reply impressed upon my spirit.

Remembering that long-ago prayer, when I'd asked for patience, I felt my pulse quicken. *Surely, Lord, you wouldn't do this to Owen just to teach me patience would you? That's not fair. That's not right.*

We placed Owen in a private Catholic preschool, where his teachers diligently worked to prepare him for kindergarten. Though it took him an extra year, he graduated to kindergarten at Makawao Elementary School.

That fall, I picked Owen up at his classroom door every afternoon. And every afternoon, his teacher pulled me aside, informing me of his behavior. It seemed that Owen preferred watching the birds outside when he was supposed to listen, got lost going to the bathroom, couldn't write or hold a pencil correctly, and became so absorbed by a thread hanging from his shorts that he couldn't do anything else until it was removed.

Most days, Owen stood next to me, listening to her reports with slumped shoulders and head down. On and on it went. Day after day after day. I tried hiding and signaling Owen to come, so I wouldn't have to face her. But she held him, waiting until I showed myself.

"I don't know how much more I can take," I grumbled to Jim in our bedroom one night. "I don't know what she expects me to do. I think I'll explode if she doesn't say something nice about Owen!"

Jim held me, letting me vent. There weren't any answers.

The next afternoon, standing at the classroom door, I braced for the day's news. Owen's teacher came over, saying he hadn't come back to class after the lunch recess bell rang.

"I found him out in the playground, hiding behind a tree, crying and covered with sand. He gave me the names of the boys who did it, and I took him to the bathroom to clean up as best he could. When he came back to class, I called all the boys outside and told Owen to 'use your biggest voice to tell them to never do this again,' which he did. Then, I asked the boys if they had anything to say, and they apologized."

Smiling, she put her hand on my arm. "When I asked Owen if he had anything to say to them, he hugged each boy and said, 'I forgive you.' "

Teary-eyed, we shared a hug.

Planning for Owen's first grade year, an Individualized Educational Program (IEP) meeting was held to determine the appropriate special education services for Owen. With his many labels—tactile sensitivity, developmental delay, anxiety disorder, low muscle tone, dyslexia, and attention deficit disorder—I looked forward to a lot of help.

At the meeting, a panel of well-dressed professionals asked his teacher if it was possible for him to learn in a classroom setting. She truthfully responded, "Yes, but he requires a tremendous amount of assistance."

No longer interested in any diagnoses or in his teacher's opinion of the difficulty of keeping Owen on track, the facilitator abruptly ended the meeting. A regular classroom was deemed the appropriate setting for Owen. He *could* learn, so he didn't require services.

Unbelievable!

Later, his teacher apologized, saying she felt she'd let us down.

"No, it wasn't you. They knew the answer they wanted and crafted their questions to hear it. I just wish they could have a day in your classroom to see the truth," I assured her. But inwardly, I wondered what to do.

Later, when I received the printed IEP, I contacted a lawyer. Looking over Owen's many issues and the Department of Education's unhelpful assessment, he recommended a lawsuit.

"You can get whatever you want for your son. What do you want?" he asked.

"Good question."

What do I want?

I wanted curriculum that met his needs and a quiet setting where he could learn at his own pace. I wanted Owen to be happy.

Thanking the lawyer for his time, I never contacted him again. I decided on what seemed like the most logical thing to do: homeschool.

While Elyse attended preschool, I worked with Owen through an amazing program called *A Bee Sees*[3]. Its weekly units based on animals, birds, and insects were broken down into daily lessons of math, language, and science. Owen, our nature lover, thrived in our quiet one-on-one environment.

I enjoyed the year but felt Owen wouldn't be "normal" if we continued homeschooling. My goal was to get him up to speed so he could successfully return to a traditional classroom setting.

By the end of first grade, Owen was reading and understanding math concepts well enough to pass an entrance exam for a small, Christian private school. We assumed the smaller class sizes would be a better fit for him than public school, and enrolled him in second grade and Elyse in kindergarten.

Elyse, ever watching and following along with Owen's lessons, already exceeded her age level for both reading and math.

In their early years, most of Owen's classmates accepted him. But, as the years went by, their acceptance turned to indifference and, eventually, annoyance. Owen, not understanding adolescent sarcasm, facial expression, or the teasing of his peers, withdrew into visual dictionaries and National Audubon Society books. Their beautiful pictures, with clear explanations beneath, provided a perfect, understandable world for Owen.

On top of poor social skills, his small stature and lack of physical ability made him even more of an outcast. Volunteering in his classes and witnessing Owen's difficulties was heart-wrenching. Owen was different.

Elyse didn't care, though. She came alongside Owen when she could, eating lunch or playing with him at recess time. Her gentle spirit and helpful nature made her a favorite amongst her teachers and classmates alike.

---

3. Hewitt Homeschooling, https://www.hewitthomeschooling.com/Elem/eBeeSees.aspx.

Still wondering why Owen was as he was, I took my concerns to a new pediatrician.

"Owen is having such a hard time in school," I fretted. "I can't help but wonder if we aren't missing something. Is there anything else we can do?"

The doctor suggested genetic testing. "I don't know if it will give us anything conclusive," she went on. "But it may reveal something we haven't yet considered."

I thanked her for offering it. At least was something.

Owen did the required blood work that day, but it took months for the results to arrive. Finally, a phone call from a geneticist gave us an answer.

"Owen has a partial trisomy of chromosome four and an inverted chromosome six. I've found studies of other abnormalities similar to either the trisomy or the inversion, but not anyone with *both*," he exclaimed.

"Wait, I need to write this down," I interrupted. "What does this mean?"

"All of Owen's issues are tied to his chromosomes. This abnormality is the reason," he explained. "Bring Owen to the clinic. I'll try and see what health risks are associated with this abnormality."

He sounded so thrilled that I thought it might be a good thing.

Taking the results of Owen's testing to school didn't bring about any changes to his individual program. The school was already addressing his educational needs to the best of their ability. So how could I force his classmates to embrace him? If I could solve that universal problem, I'd be a bazillionaire.

Near the end of his fifth-grade year, when I came to pick him and Elyse up after school, I found Owen crying under a bench. He couldn't adequately describe what was so upsetting, but his tears confirmed what I dreaded. Owen needed quiet, simple support in order to learn. He needed to learn at home.

When Jim and I decided to homeschool eleven-year-old Owen, we gave nine-year-old Elyse the option to either continue in school or be homeschooled.

Without a moment's hesitation, she said, "Homeschool!"

I smiled inwardly at her quick choice of *me* as her teacher, but the real reason soon became apparent. Elyse's hatred of morning, especially the required *early* morning for school, played the largest part in her decision. Thoughts of rolling out of bed midmorning and starting the day in pajamas thrilled her.

Once the decision was made to homeschool *both* children, fear sank in. Was I capable of educating them? With only a high school diploma, what made me think I could complete their education? Or shape them to become successful, contributing members of society?

Turning to Google, I typed in "best homeschool curriculum" and pulled up over six million hits. *That's nuts.* Looking for help, I joined a local homeschool group and flew to Oahu for an inspirational conference.

As I walked through a gymnasium filled with vendors pitching their products, I prayed for God's direction. Overwhelmed by the task ahead, I selected an all-in-one unit studies program, with a forty-week preprinted and preplanned schedule that would guide a novice like me.

The Tuesday after Labor Day, we began our first school day by standing and singing the National Anthem and "Hawai'i Ponoi" (our state anthem). We then recited the Pledge of Allegiance to the tiny American flag on our wall. Watching the tiny Americans beside me, I smiled. *This is so cool!*

After a couple of weeks, though, all that patriotism grated on our nerves. Satisfied that we could hold our own at the start of any sporting event, I dropped the practice.

Striving to complete everything in our neatly packaged

program left little time for anything else. By the end of the second week, we were already behind and started working late into the evenings to keep up. I was frustrated and so were the children.

Maybe homeschooling wasn't such a good idea.

But we fought through that first year, dropping redundant math problems and excessive writing lessons. At year's end, when we did standardized testing, both children tested in the average and above-average ranges. Victory!

As the years ticked by, Elyse, who had been such an easy baby, was also an easy student. Loving the scent and feel of a new workbook, she devoured lessons in Latin and Greek word roots, literature, and history, quickly surpassing her teacher's knowledge.

When we watched her favorite TV show, *Jeopardy*, Jim and I couldn't compete with her knowledge. For high school, we placed her in a challenging online program, which was a good fit academically but left her lonely in front of a computer screen day after day.

Owen hated workbooks and all the laborious handwriting they demanded. He couldn't retain information simply by reading a textbook passage and answering corresponding questions. So his education became a hodgepodge of anything that might possibly cover a core requirement.

For him, we used *Mad Libs*, *Movies as Literature*[4], and textbooks with accompanying audio CDs. And we did lots of oral exams. Grateful that I didn't have to explain my choices to "real" educators, I found his test scores proved that it was working. Hallelujah!

---

4. Kathryn L. Stout and Richard B. Stout, *Movies as Literature*, Design-A-Study, retrieved April 25, 2017, http://www.designastudy. com/products/1891975099.html.

I thoroughly enjoyed learning with the kids. Some days were better than others, but overall I treasured our time together and wouldn't have traded it for any paycheck. Except maybe at the end of the month when all the bills came in.

Despite Elyse and Owen's academic success, I kept wondering if homeschooling would make them weird. Our extended family was supportive, but the world at large looked on with skepticism. When out in public with the children, I'd occasionally have to field the dreaded question of why they weren't in school.

"Holiday today?"

"No, we homeschool," I'd smile, bracing for the next inevitable question.

"Homeschool, huh? Well, what do you do for socialization?"

"Oh, we take classes with other homeschooled children and do field trips together." This answer often received a satisfactory nod. One homeschool parent's humorous suggestion to answer with "I put them in the bathroom and beat them for their lunch money" often crossed my mind, but I was never brave enough to try it out.

Elyse developed friendships with other homeschooled children, but Owen didn't possess the desire or skill to maintain friends. Elyse was his best friend and that was enough for him. Owen never felt sorry for himself, though. He arose each day with a smile on his face and a general trust in humankind that worried me.

But I shouldn't have worried.

When the kids were young teens, we vacationed in Disneyland, with a one-day pass to Disney's California Adventure park. Owen's one request was to ride the roller coaster California Screamin', which we assured him we'd ride before the day's end.

"We'll ride the roller coaster, right?" he kept reminding us.

"Yes, Owen. Don't worry."

Near the end of the day as we headed toward the ride, we spotted workers walking up near the top of the coaster's largest loop.

Oh no.

The ride wasn't running. We stopped in at a nearby shop, asking an employee, "Do you think it will reopen?"

Shaking his head, the helpful fellow stated, "Being so close to the end of the day, they'll probably just leave it closed."

Owen's face fell.

"Oh Owen, I'm so sorry! We should have ridden it first thing today," I moaned and tried to hug him.

"Oh well." He shrugged, wiping his eyes.

"Let's pray," I suggested. Stepping outside, we gathered on the edge of the sidewalk and closed our eyes. "Lord, you can do anything. Please open this ride for Owen. Amen."

Opening our eyes, we saw a car from the ride suddenly speed by on an overhead track!

"Come on, Owen! Let's go!"

"Elyse and I will wait back here," Jim called as Owen and I ran to the ride, praying all the way.

"Lord, please let the ride be open. Help us get there in time!" I panted as our tennis shoes thumped along the boardwalk fronting the ride.

"Yes, Lord," Owen puffed behind me.

Nearing the entrance of the ride, we saw no line, but we also saw no sign saying it was closed. Running in, we climbed the stairs, arriving at the end of a strangely short line.

"Do you want to ride in the front car, Owen?"

"Yeah."

We entered the gate for the front car and overheard an employee telling the people behind us, "You'll have to take another position. We will only be running the ride a few more times, and all the front row seats are filled."

Smiling at Owen, I whispered, "See? God not only opened the ride, he gave you the front seat!"

"I want a blue car," Owen stated. "Can we pray for a blue car?"

What? Are you nuts? Be grateful for all God has done! God doesn't have time for this.

"Okay, Owen." Bowing our heads once more, I quietly began, "Lord, we thank you for getting us here. Thank you that the ride opened and that we can ride in front. If it's your will, please let our car be blue. If not, we'll ride whatever car it is, and be happy about it, but we would love a blue car. Amen."

"Amen." Owen smiled.

"You know that we will have to ride whatever color car comes, right?"

"I know."

Watching the couple in front of us get into an orange car, adrenaline coursed through my veins. Seeing our car in the distance, I laughed aloud. It was *blue*!

"You are sure loved by the Lord, Owen."

12

SLOWLY FASTING

The kids were growing into great adults, the bills were paid, and my marriage was stable. From all appearances, I should have been a champion of satisfaction and contentment. Instead, I felt guilty that I ached for something more. Just what that something *was* was a mystery.

I suspected that it had something to do with my spiritual life, but how could that be? I checked all the boxes in what seemed the perfect formula for God's approval and blessing. I read my Bible through every year, homeschooled the kids, volunteered to count the offering after church, and ran the sermon's PowerPoint slides once a month.

Jim still made copies of the sermons, graduating from cassette tapes to CDs these two decades after my stalking him. Owen helped in Sunday school, Elyse was active in her youth group, and we even had weekly Bible studies in our home.

It all should have earned a "bravo!" from above as far as I was concerned.

Still, I felt distant from God.

What was wrong with me?

Exercise. That must be what I need. Pulling out my old sneakers, I added a brisk walk to the daily routine. Preferring to walk in the cool early morning, I'd rise at 4:45, read my Bible, (because God was first), walk, rush home to make breakfast, rouse Jim, and throw his lunch in a sack by the time he left at 6:50. I could almost hear the ticking clock in my brain.

By 8:00, our supposed homeschool starting time, I was ready to go back to bed. After lunch, while the kids read history or literature aloud, I often fell asleep, waking to their giggles. Popping in a video was a guaranteed snooze fest. Within weeks, the 4:45 a.m. wake-up time, along with the exercise, was booted into oblivion.

Of course, since I was a married woman, any emptiness I felt must be my husband's fault, right? Surely, if he took me on more dates or bought me flowers or candy or jewelry, then I'd be happy like those perfect couples in the TV commercials.

But with our tight single-income budget, I knew these were unnecessary extravagances. I'd have to suffer silently. Sometimes I'd make Jim suffer with the silent treatment.

Maybe I needed to seek counsel. Yikes. Wasn't that for people with big issues? Was dissatisfaction reason enough to gain an audience with my pastor?

While I liked Pastor Dale a lot, he wasn't one to settle on simply making me feel good about myself. He'd probably get down to business and ask tough questions to unearth the reason for my poor attitude.

What if my problem was me?

Still, I couldn't shake the feeling that this hunger for something more had to do with God. My logical "do this and get that" image of God wasn't panning out. So who was God?

Was he the God of the Old Testament? Strong and terrible? Holy and just? Striking cities with plagues and death? Ordering kings to annihilate whole cities?

Or was he Jesus? The God-man who came to show us love and taught about forgiveness and grace?

Familiar with the Trinity—Father, Son, and Holy Spirit—I knew God was all of this, and yet all this thinking about God started an inward shift. I no longer wanted to just please God. I wanted to know him. I just didn't know how.

In church one sunny Sunday morning, I gazed out the window at the familiar green pastures, pine trees, and deep valleys of Haleakala. Waipuna Chapel, the same church that had supported me during my teen pregnancy, held the comfort of well-worn jeans.

But today, sitting in the same second-from-the-back row, with the same people, and the same view, I sighed deeply, still aching for change.

I guess it'll be Antiques Roadshow *again after church, and a nap on the couch. What'll we do for lunch? I have a loaf of bread. Maybe grilled cheese.*

Pastor Dale's message about life dreams, called "Wide Awake," drifted into my lunch plans. Speaking on the importance of dreams as fuel for our lives, he asked, "What do you want to see God do in your own life?"

That's just it. I don't know what I want. Well, I don't want to mess up. And I want to travel. But that takes money.

His stirring questions continued. "Sometimes we fall asleep in our dreams. What keeps us asleep?"

He started listing reasons why we don't pursue our dreams. Money ranked second. *Yep.* Another reason was fear of making a mistake. *Hmm, I'm not the only one.* Intrigued, I started scribbling notes on my bulletin.

"All of us are meant for a life of significance . . ."

Really? Looking up at Dale, my eyes narrowed and my pen stopped.

My life's goal of not being a disappointment hadn't worked out. But *significance*? Ha! Now there was a long shot.

Envisioning my grand entry into heaven, I imagined God, shining brightly on his glorious throne and surrounded by the heavenly host, slowly shaking his head. "You know, Eileen, I had a great plan for you, and you totally missed it. Life could have been so much more." Standing with shoulders slumped and head hung low, I'd beg to stay and scrub the golden toilets.

"Your dreams are God's way of whispering into your soul," Dale concluded. "There is more to you than you know . . . an extraordinary life awaiting you if you would just trust God."

Extraordinary? As a homeschooling mom, my dreams centered on clean laundry, washed dishes, and written lesson plans. Nothing very significant or extraordinary there.

And weren't dreams just for young children who wanted to be firefighters or ballerinas when they grew up? What happened when mistakes changed the course of our lives? Didn't we have to just keep going? Trudge through the reality of how life played out?

But Dale's sermon made it sound like dreams were a *good* thing. Like something that God could use to reveal possibilities we'd never considered, or maybe even our life's purpose. And it sounded like dreams could happen *now,* despite age or circumstance.

Oh man, I want one!

So just what would a good God-fearing, life-changing dream be like? With no hobbies or interests (other than napping) I had . . . nothing.

What was wrong with me?

If dreams were God's way of whispering into my soul, I was deaf.

Discouraged by my lack of spirituality, I searched for an ideal dream. With my children getting older and homeschool graduation on the horizon, what was next? Go back to work and replace our depleted savings? Go to school and earn the degree I'd always wanted? Neither seemed very enticing or extraordinary.

I wanted a dream. I *needed* a dream. Not *a* dream, but *the* dream. It would have to be BIG, and life changing, and make no sense, but be something that would make God take notice. I could almost hear him say, "Well done, good and faithful servant," when I decided we needed to sell our home. *Yes!* Oh, what freedom that would afford! We could do whatever God wanted, with a big wad of cash in our pocket! We could be missionaries! We could travel, or help others, or start a soup kitchen, or take care of orphans. Endless possibilities!

Funny thing, but when I brought this awe-inspiring dream to Jim, it didn't bode well with him. Silently staring at me over the top of the newspaper he'd been reading, he listened as I gushed on and on about all the good we could do when we sold the house.

Slowly folding the paper when I finally quieted, he set it aside. Crossing his arms across his chest, he leaned back in his chair, informing me, "I like to know where I'm sleeping at night."

"Yeah, I do too." Looking at the floor, I felt my face flush.

"And I thought we agreed to leave this place to the kids when we're gone," he reminded me. *True, we had talked about that eons ago.* And I had to admit it seemed like something that would also please God.

"You're right." Deflated, I turned away, muttering to heaven, "If you have a dream for me, would you please give it to Jim too?" After nineteen years of marriage, I'd learned no amount of cajoling could make Jim do anything he didn't want to do. This dream was dead on arrival.

The following week, Pastor Dale continued his series on the importance of dreams. Hiding behind the person in front of me, I hoped Dale couldn't see my irritation. *Surely this sermon was meant for someone. Just not for me.*

When church finally ended, I made my way outside and bumped into my friends Sylvia and Carla.

"Let's meet downstairs on Thursday afternoon," Sylvia was saying.

"Okay, that'll work for me," Carla agreed.

"Hey," I interrupted. "What's up?"

"Oh, we're just talking about the fast we're going to do." Grabbing my arm, Sylvia smiled and her eyes brightened. "You should totally do this with us! Me, Carla, Sharon, and Theresa are going to do it."

"Um, I'm not much of a faster." Crinkling my nose, I strategically stretched out of Sylvia's grip.

"It's not a total fast. You can still eat. It's called a 'Daniel Fast.' You know, Daniel from the Bible? He prayed for twenty-one days and didn't eat anything special. Just vegetables and water," she explained. "It's a way to draw closer to God."

"I'm not a faster either," Carla said. "But this is doable. Google it and see what you think."

"Okay. When are you guys starting?"

"Tomorrow," Carla answered.

Tomorrow?

"I'll keep it in mind." Seeing Jim waiting for me, I excused myself. What was I getting myself into? But I hadn't committed. I could easily tell them I wasn't prepared and let it go.

Then again, maybe it would give me a dream.

At home, sitting in front of the computer, my search for the "Daniel Fast" pulled up several hits on the web. Musing on its craziness, I found it consisted more of what *not* to eat than what *to* eat. The premise for the entire fast came from one short verse in the Bible:

All that time I had eaten no rich food.
No meat or wine crossed my lips,
and I used no fragrant lotions until those
three weeks had passed.

—Daniel 10:3 (NLT)

The interpretation was that Daniel only ate foods derived from soil and drank only water. *Doesn't sound so bad.* The "fragrant lotions" of ancient days were used for skin care and odor. Mercifully, no one suggested giving up deodorant. Eventually, I sorted out a list of dietary deletions:

- no sugar, agave, honey, or any form of sweetener
- no caffeine of any sort
- no fried foods
- no yeast or anything made with yeast
- no animal anything
- no juice or wine
- no chocolate
- no fun

Everything had to be plant based and whole grain, preferably organic, with no refinement of any kind. Recipes for weird, healthy foods were on the web, but I didn't have any of the listed ingredients. I'd have to go shopping right away and start reading food labels.

Impressed by my friends' desire to know God more through fasting, and wanting to be just as spiritual, I nevertheless knew it would be an enormous challenge. And what about Jim? Would he laugh at me?

Do I really want to do this?

Leaning back in my chair, I stared at the ceiling. *What's the worst that could happen?*

I guess nothing.

But what if something did happen?

Shoot, I might even lose some weight or feel healthier.

With a goal of becoming more mindful in prayer and drawing nearer to God, I whispered, "God, I don't know what I'm doing. If this is a good plan, then help me do it."

With a deep sigh, I put together a simple list, and went to Costco for supplies.

Starting the fast the next day, I found that food occupied my every thought. I'd no sooner finish one meal than start worrying about the next. The first day's menu consisted of oatmeal with almond milk, plain rice crackers and peanut butter, brown rice, and soybeans. A bit of fruit rounded out the day. Dropping into bed that evening, I rejoiced that one day was done. Only twenty more to go.

This doesn't feel very spiritual.

At our weekly encouragement meetings, the other women reported strengthened marriages, healing of past hurts, and demolished strongholds. But I was a fasting misfit. All I thought about was *food*.

I missed my trips to the pantry, where chocolate and potato chips beckoned for any mood swings or boredom. I prayed and asked God, "What is this all about? Why am I doing this?" But I was given no answer. No burning bush. No voice from above.

Even though I felt physically better near the end of the fast, having lost seven pounds, and experiencing fewer premenopausal hot flashes, I still felt empty.

Weight loss and less sweat? Am I really that shallow?

Finally, kneeling in my bedroom on the last day of the fast, I begged, "God, I know there's a reason for this. Nothing is wasted in your economy. Please, give me an answer. What was this about?"

"*Preparation.*" A single word was impressed upon my spirit. Preparation? For what? Mission work where there is no food? Famine?

At our last meeting, I shared this strange revelation with my fasting friends. They were as confused as me over the meaning. But we were done.

Kaggy, a mainland friend who hadn't participated in the fast, asked over the phone, "What did you get out of it?" Sharing my one word, she mused, "Huh, I wonder what that's all about."

At year's end, when the holiday season began, I promptly forgot all about *preparation*. As I returned to normal food and my old routine, those seven pounds also returned, bringing friends.

13

LONGING FOR GOD

W hat does it take to know you, Lord?"
Alone one cool January morning, with New Year's resolutions and the desire for change hanging heavy in the air, I knelt against my old, brown chair, enjoying the stillness of a sleeping household, letting my prayers wander.

A long-ago walk up the street with toddler Owen came to mind.

Laughing, with tiny hands raised in his striped blue stroller, Owen squealed, "Pupu falloos," as I rained handfuls of purple flowers over his head. A neighbor's Jacaranda tree covered the ground with the fragile lavender blooms. The morning sun sparkled between the rustling green leaves above us, in a powder-blue, cloudless sky.

Thank you, God. Thank you for trees and flowers and senses to enjoy it all.

Owen's delight in such simple gestures made me laugh. Though his development was a tedious process, he was always ready to take on the day. His pleasure at simply *being* spoke volumes to me, making me think that everyone needed to be more like him, instead of trying to make him more like everyone else.

As we continued our stroll, a gentle voice asked, *"What's a soul worth?"*

Glancing behind me but seeing no one, I felt a sudden, strange affection surge for the unknown souls behind the closed doors of my street.

A soul's worth? Everything, Lord. I'd give anything for a soul to be spared hell. I'd give my money, my time . . . I'd give my life if need be.

I shuddered at that last thought as the feeling waned. Doubts taunted: *Could you really give your life for a stranger? For someone who despised you?*

What an imagination! Shaking my head, I turned my thoughts back to the day at hand. *Let's see. What do I need to do today? Laundry. Yes, laundry.*

Picking up the pace, I hurried home.

I squirmed against my chair. Though I'd often wondered about that question, I had no answer.

Trying to resume my rote prayer list of "Bless Grammy, cover Jim, protect Brandon, guide Owen, strengthen Elyse," I again veered away, venturing further into unknown territory.

"Lord, what do you want from me? Do you want my money?" Still on my knees, I filed through a mental list of easily relinquished pieces—nice-to-have, replaceable things.

"You can have them, Lord, for your use—our finances, house, cars—I give them freely back to you. Do with them as you choose." Picturing Jim's horrified face as I gave everything away gave me pause.

Was I crazy?

It seemed too easy, though, like it wasn't enough.

"Is it my time you want?" No audible answer came.

What if God wanted more than my finite, material things? More than my accomplishments or what I could do for him? What if God wanted my family?

Breathing heavier, I wondered what that would mean. "Do you really want me to give you my family?" I whispered, tears filling my eyes at the thought of losing them.

"I love them, Lord, but you love them even more than I'm able. You see them when I can't and only you can guide their steps." Reaching for a tissue, I blew my nose.

Why is this so hard? If he's God, then I'd be foolish not to entrust them to him.

But they're mine. Jim is my husband, and they're my kids. I want to be in charge.

"God, I know you're GOD, but I need faith to trust you in this." Would they be taken from me? *Please God, no.*

This is ridiculous. God doesn't require a conscious giving over of family, does he? What am I doing?

Well, Abraham was asked to give his beloved son Isaac. On an altar. As a sacrifice.

But that was the Old Testament. That doesn't happen today. There are laws preventing such abuse.

God is God, though. Can't I trust him? Even if I'm mistaken in my approach, he'd understand my desire to know him.

Do it. Trust God.

Hoping for a sign that I was moving in the right direction, I waited. The moment felt as charged as a brewing storm right before lightning strikes.

Finally, I gave in. "Okay, Lord. I love them so much, but only you can see their thoughts and keep them safe. I want them to know you and serve you." Pulse quickening, I exhaled. "I give them all to you. Have your way in my family."

Deep relief, sprinkled with doubt and a dash of fear, filled my soul. An irrepressible urge began thickening like a huge wave, propelling me further still. Not wanting to miss it, I paddled furiously into the apex, pushing myself over. I threw my hands in the air, laughing, as if barreling down a massive wall of water with the sun on my face and the wind in my hair. *I'd give God everything!*

"God, I give you all of me. I don't want to hold on or hold back. I give you my life. Have your way in me. Bring glory to yourself through my life. It's yours."

Tears coursing down my cheeks, hands rising in complete surrender, face smiling up to the heavens, joy filling my very being—truly, this was the new beginning I'd sought.

Lowering my hands, I heaved a deep, satisfied sigh, basking in this moment of sincere release. God would have his way in my life.

Then, four little words shattered the stillness.

"What about your health?"

My health? What? *No!* The wave I'd ridden crashed, engulfing me, rolling me over and over in the white wash.

Quickly standing, with my hands stretched wide open as if trying to catch myself from falling, I heard my heart pounding in my head.

"No! Not my health!" Turning, I fled to the kitchen. Willing my body to begin the day, I stood gripping the kitchen counter, trying to breathe and make sense of what had just happened.

This can't be real. God doesn't do things like that. God is a giver of good things. Not illness. Not death. Why would he ask for my health? I'd been searching for a dream, not a nightmare.

Paralyzed by fear, sweat built on my brow, I tried to soothe myself. *Calm down; it's just your imagination.* I glanced at the clock; the time pressed for action. Breakfast called.

Oatmeal, soft-boiled egg, coffee . . . on to Jim's lunch, sandwich, cut an apple, fill the paper bag . . . set the table for breakfast, wake Jim.

"Morning, hon. Time to get up," I called, opening our bedroom door.

"Mmmhmm," he groaned. His relaxed form snuggled under the covers made me want to crawl back into bed and restart this awful day.

Fifteen minutes later, Jim joined me at the table. He blessed our food, and we ate in silence.

"You're quiet today," he observed, missing my normal chatter about my plans for the day.

"Yeah, just thinking about all I need to do today," I lied.

What about your health? Over and over the words replayed in my head.

The oatmeal stuck in my throat. *What if this is real?* Tears pricked the corners of my eyes, threatening to rain down my cheeks. Longing to share with Jim but fearing his ridicule, I chose to wrestle alone. *He'll think I'm nuts. Maybe I AM nuts.*

Breakfast done, we piled the dishes in the sink. I absently rinsed them as Jim returned to the bedroom to get ready for work.

God, I wanted to know you more, to draw closer to you. Not to be sick! Am I going to die?

Immediately, I was transported back to the day I found Dad's lifeless body.

I had arrived at our family home in Haiku, still in my postal uniform, after a half day of work. Mom, Eleanor, and Gordon sat around the dining table, eating sandwiches. I slipped into a chair alongside them, joining their quiet chatter. Dad lay comatose in his back bedroom, as he'd been for weeks.

Suddenly, he let out a loud moan, startling me.

"Should I go and check on him?" I asked. They chuckled a bit and said not to worry. He'd been moaning that way all morning.

A few minutes later, I excused myself to go down the hall and sit with Dad. Entering his room, I found him lying completely still, eyes open and fixed, mouth askew, and tongue unnaturally curled upward.

Gasping, I ran back to the dining room. "I think he's gone!" Eleanor sprang up, knocking over her chair. We all hurried back to the bedroom, taking in the sight of Dad's body. With tears in her eyes, Mom calmly said, "Yes, he's gone."

Shuddering at the memory, I reasoned that God didn't say he *would* take my health, or that I *would* die. Was this simply a test of faith? Something like the time God asked Abraham to offer Isaac on the altar and then, at the last moment, provided a different way? Would God provide a different way for me? Surely seeking to draw closer to God couldn't mean illness.

Then again, what if illness was the catalyst to knowing him? What if it was something that would deepen my family's faith? What if God really *did* use things like illness and death?

In ancient Egypt, God sent the Angel of Death to kill the firstborn of Egypt. He'd used plagues, snakes, and all sorts of awful things back then. Weren't these used for punishment, though? I *sought* God. This made no sense.

Oh God, this is too big for me. I want to know you, but I don't want to be sick. Isn't there another way?

Later that morning, pulling out my Bible, I read about Jesus. I knew he'd struggled in the garden the night before his death. Rereading how he begged God three different times, "If there is any other way, take this from me," I felt a twinge of his agony.

But each time he had asked, he submitted his own will to his Father, saying, "Your will be done." Apparently, there was no other way.

But I wouldn't submit. Like Jonah, I ran from God. When God told Jonah to prophesy his judgment on the city of Nineveh, Jonah hopped the first ship in the opposite direction. The poor sailors of that ship! God sent a storm that nearly sank the vessel, until they threw Jonah overboard. It took a near drowning, then a long weekend in the belly of a whale, for Jonah to change his mind.

A whale-sized storm quickly swallowed my mind. Favorite pastimes of watching television, eating, and reading proved meaningless. Though I felt exhausted, sleep was elusive. I'd lay in bed, listening to Jim's heavy breathing, wondering what would happen when I was gone. Who would pay the bills? Take the cat to the vet? Rub Elyse's back when she was sad? Encourage Owen?

Will he remarry?

Stop it! You don't know what will happen.

Over the next five days, the mind battle raged. I tried to balance the checkbook but kept transposing numbers. I'd open my email and close it again. I didn't care who posted what on Facebook. My Bible sat idle.

Reading lessons with Owen or correcting a math page for Elyse, I'd watch them, wondering how they would manage without me. Owen was nearly done with high school; what would he do next? Elyse had a couple of years to go but was afraid to consider leaving Maui for college. Who would help her find her way?

I gave up kneeling at my chair. I didn't want to pray. I didn't want to face that question. All I could think about was dying. Up until now, I'd been complaining about getting older. Now I ached to get old.

While I thought I wanted to give God all, I wanted to be *here.* If I gave God my health, I'd have no control. But did I *really* have any control in this life? Did anyone?

Finally, in the wee hours of a cool morning, I snuck out of our bedroom. On my knees, I again leaned against the old, brown chair at my desk.

"Lord, I don't want to die. I want to be here for Jim and the kids. I want to see them marry and have children of their own. And what about Mom? I want to be here to care for her too." *Mom.* My breath came out in a whimper. At eighty-one, she needed me.

"God, I know you're God. I don't understand what you want or why you're asking for my health, but I choose to trust you. I trust you with it all. You can have my health."

Though no "Hallelujah Chorus" rang out, a deep peace washed away the turmoil in my soul. I'd done the right thing.

Another more ominous sense, like that of strapping on the seat belt of a radical, terrifying, roller-coaster ride, also blanketed me. But this ride didn't have a safe and secure ending.

Illness was coming.

14

WAITING FOR TRUTH

In the weeks that followed, my thoughts bounced between blindly accepting God's plan of illness and denying that God would make me (or anyone, for that matter) sick. *What could possibly be the endgame to that?* I shuddered to think.

And how in the world would I tell Jim? "Hey, honey, God asked for my health, and I said, 'Go ahead and take it!' " He'd be calling the white coats for sure.

In the shower at night, I thought up great speeches about illness and faith to share with the world, should I survive. I imagined pointing at my audience and hearing their laughter as I joked about being very careful of what you pray for.

But maybe this was all just a misunderstanding that I was blowing out of proportion.

At forty-five, I was too young to die. My kids were nearly grown, but not quite. We'd traveled a bit, but not enough. My passport's pages bore not a single stamp. Would there be time?

Get a grip, Eileen! Instead of basking in death, find something to do while you feel good!

I found myself thinking up projects, so Owen and Elyse would have something to remember me by, just in case I didn't make it. Working my way through their closets and childhood memorabilia, I started cleaning, repainting, and updating their rooms. *I'll get new bedding and drapes, maybe some shelving and artwork. It should last them a few years.*

Frowning at my reflection in the mirror one morning, I saw that my Natural Instincts number ten was fading, leaving a silver streak down the center of my scalp. *Well, if it's just going to fall out anyway, I might as well get a jump on it.*

Assuming that colorless hair would be easier to lose than my shoulder-length, dark blonde waves, I decided to "go natural" (code for gray) and cut it short. No longer would I have to deal with root lines or worry about Walmart running out of my color. I'd be free!

In the quiet moments between home improvement projects and changing hairstyles, time kept passing, but nothing bad materialized. I began to wonder if maybe these thoughts of illness and dying were just my imagination in premenopausal-drama mode.

One cool February night, I lay in bed, feeling a bit bloated and rubbing my stomach. A small, hard lump on my left side surprised me. I pressed harder, and fear rippled over my body. *Probably just my bowels. I'll see what it feels like in the morning.*

Sure enough, by morning it was gone. But I began a new ritual of rubbing my belly in bed before falling asleep. Some days I'd find the lump, and other days I wouldn't. *I must need more fiber in my diet.*

The weeks rolled by with the lump taunting me. *God, this can't be real. Surely you wouldn't do something like this. Please, make it go away.*

By April, as I struggled to zip up my shorts, I knew something was wrong. Really wrong. One night, as Jim and I lay in bed with the lights off, waiting for sleep to come, I rolled over and faced him. "Can you feel this?"

"Hmmm? What'd you say?"

"Give me your hand."

Reaching over, I took his hand, pressing his fingers into my abdomen.

"What's that?!"

"I don't know," I moaned. "I'm hoping it's just my bowels."

He can feel it. It's real.

"It's really hard! You need to get that thing checked."

"I know."

He was right, but I felt paralyzed. Confirmation was too hard to imagine.

More weeks of cleaning, painting, and planning flew by. I did anything to avoid going in and getting checked. But Jim was on to me. Lying in bed one warm June evening, he chided, "You can't lie on your back anymore, and I see you struggling to wash dishes. Do you even realize that you're turning sideways at the sink?"

"I know, Jim. I know."

Feeling his frustration, but unable to see his face in the darkness, I breathed my biggest fear, "I'm afraid it could be lymphoma."

The ugly word hung in the still air.

"Even so, you need to know. You've put it off long enough." His practicality, unfazed by my fear, made perfect sense. Strangely, it gave me strength.

"Okay. You're right. I'll call in the morning," I promised.

The next morning, staring at the phone in my hand, I took a deep breath, and quickly dialed the clinic. My primary care physician, Dr. Talbot, wasn't available, but fearing I'd lose my nerve, I warily agreed to see a new doctor, Dr. Smithson, the next day, Thursday, June 23.

"She's a good doctor," the receptionist assured me. "I've seen her myself."

At the appointment, sitting on the exam table, I mentioned the abundance of fiber in my diet.

Briefly pressing my abdomen, she exclaimed, "You're full of gas!"

Gas? Really?

Unconvinced, I told her about the lump.

"Where is it?"

"It seems to move but is generally around here," I answered pointing at my upper abdomen.

"I want you to stop all fiber and take Prilosec for ten days," she advised turning to her computer and tapping in her notes. We were done.

Lingering at the door a moment, not satisfied with her findings, I searched for something to say. Trying to get past me, she stuck out her hand saying, "Call me if you have any further problems."

"You know, I was afraid this was lymphoma. My dad died from it and said that none of his family lived to see fifty." I'd said it. I voiced the ugly word.

Tilting her head to one side, she reiterated, "This is just gas. If you still have problems after the Prilosec, then call me."

"All right. I will. Thank you."

Either she's a great doctor, or she has no idea what's going on.

After three days on Prilosec with no fiber, I felt worse than ever. Nonexistent bowel movements left me extremely bloated and absolutely miserable. I called the clinic and left messages, but it took a few days to arrange a phone appointment. Finally, the doctor decided to proceed with a CT scan.

"I'll call in the order, and they'll call you to schedule the appointment."

"Okay. How long does that normally take?"

"They should call you within a day or two."

A week later, I called the CT department.

"Hi. This is Eileen Kusakabe. I was supposed to be contacted for a scan ordered by Dr. Smithson."

"Okay, let me check," replied a cheerful man's voice.

After a few seconds, he stated that he had an order from an unfamiliar doctor.

"That can't be right. I don't know who that doctor is. The order was supposed to be from Dr. Smithson."

"Hmmm . . ." Feverish typing sounded in my ear.

"Can I put you on a brief hold?" he asked.

"Sure."

Eventually, he returned, explaining that my doctor had placed an incorrect order, and the doctor I hadn't seen had corrected the order. "Would you like to come in right away?" he continued. "First available appointment?"

Why the sudden rush?

"Okay, sounds good to me." We scheduled it for the following Tuesday, July 26.

Three days before the CT scan, on Saturday, July 23, our extended family enjoyed a beach day at Kamaole III in Kihei. All my siblings and their families came to see Brandon, who was visiting from school in California. Even Mom, who doesn't particularly like the ocean, came for the day.

Sunlight danced on the glassy ocean that morning, drawing many into the water. Kathleen's son, John, mercilessly fired a water gun with sniper-like precision. Brandon, blocking the onslaught with a boogie board, raced to catch him. Eleanor and Kathleen stood watching and laughing in the shallows.

Eleanor's husband, Gary, built sandcastles on the shore with their grown son, Aaron, and little grandson, Isaac. Jim, Owen, and Elyse raced with boogie boards in hand for the next big wave. I gazed at the family from off shore, feeling the familiar lump pressed against my boogie board as I rested beyond the surf break.

I should tell them . . . but it'll ruin the day. Besides, if I'm wrong, I'll look like a fool.

Remaining silent, I savored the day.

After church the next day, I dragged Jim and the kids out to the backyard for our annual Christmas photo. Though early this year, it was the only time we could include Brandon, as he was heading back to California on Monday. Jim, standing in front of an avocado tree, waited while Brandon, Owen, and Elyse climbed up and sat on a branch behind him. Setting the camera's timer, I darted next to Jim.

As the family groaned with each take, I cherished the moment. *This could be my last Christmas.*

Tuesday, the day of the scan, I was sound asleep and dreaming. Sensing morning was near, my dreams started fading as a tall, brilliant, beautiful light appeared.

Jesus!

Instantly recognizing him, I was surprised that I felt no fear, only incredible peace. Gazing at this radiating figure of a man, without defined features, I heard four simple words:

"They will find nothing."

Gasping, I suddenly found myself back in my room. Disappointed as I looked around at the walls and ceiling, I wanted to go back and be with Jesus. Breathing deeply, heart pounding, I kept turning the vision over and over in my mind.

They will find nothing? Had I really cut my hair, cleaned and painted bedrooms, and worried myself sick about dying for nothing? Was it a mistake thinking God had asked for my health?

Shaking my head at the foolishness of *wanting* something to be found, I laughed at myself.

Jesus had come to me and spoken to me. *Me*, of all people. With the worrisome scan scheduled in just a few hours, calmness settled. After all, they'd find nothing, right?

Later that morning, as Jim dressed for work, I sat on our bed telling him of my Jesus dream.

Cocking his head to one side, he shrugged. "Let's hope it's true."

15

AN UNWANTED ANSWER

Down at the Kaiser Clinic a few hours later, a friendly receptionist presented me with twelve ounces of banana-flavored barium to drink. Choking down the sweetened chalk, I walked around the clinic waiting the required two hours for it to settle.

My stomach gurgled as the two-hour mark drew near. Running to the public restroom and pushing into a stall, I quickly sat while involuntary bowel movements erupted. Embarrassed as other women in the restroom quickly exited, I worried that I'd blown the test—literally. Was a CT scan something like a pregnancy ultrasound where you're required to drink a lot of water and hold it until they're done? I hoped not.

Hobbling back to the lab, I confessed to the tech what had happened. With a smile, he assured me, "Everything that needs to be in there is in there." Handing me another four ounces of the chalk to top off my innards, he then inserted an IV tube into my arm for a contrast agent. After I swallowed the last grainy bits, he handed me a paper gown.

Soon I was alone, settled on a cold metal table with a huge donut-shaped scanner at my feet. Soon I would know the truth.

"We'll do a practice scan," the tech's friendly voice floated in from behind a windowed wall, "and then finish with the contrast. It might feel a little warm when it goes in, but just call if anything is uncomfortable. Are you ready?"

"Yes."

The donut began spinning. "Deep breath . . . hold it . . . release," a mechanical voice commanded as the table slid my midsection through the whirring donut.

"Are you doing all right?"

"I'm fine."

"Okay. One more pass with the contrast, and we'll be done."

The table moved me through again, this time with heat radiating down my groin, making me feel as if I was wetting myself. The whole test took fewer than twenty minutes.

In silence, the lab tech stood at my side, removing the IV, no longer making eye contact.

"Can you tell me anything?"

Looking at his hands, he twisted the pen he held. "You need to call your doctor for the results."

"Oh, okay. I didn't think you could tell me anything."

After waiting outside while I changed back into my clothes, he walked me out, staring at the floor. "Your doctor will have the results this afternoon." Glancing up at me, he urged, "Call her then for the results."

Heart skipping a beat, I looked away.

In the distance, another technician spoke with the receptionist in hushed tones, quieting with our approach.

"Thank you so much," I said, smiling.

But no smile was returned. Just a simple nod. *Was that pity in their eyes?*

Walking out of the clinic, I bumped into a friend who candidly asked why I was there. Answering casually, "Twenty-thousand-mile checkup," I couldn't give validity to my feelings of impending doom. But she sensed something was wrong and began praying for me.

That afternoon, I refused to call the doctor. *If she's got something to say, she can call me.* By evening, the phone hadn't rung. Jim came home from work, asking if I'd heard anything. I shook my head. "Nope, must be okay. No news is good news, right?"

As we sat down for our spaghetti dinner just after 6:00, the phone rang. Pushing my chair back, I snatched up the nearest handset. "Hello?"

"Mrs. Kusakabe, this is Dr. Smithson. I have the results of your CT scan."

Hurrying to our bedroom, I shut the door behind me. "And . . . ?"

"It seems you have a swollen lymph node in your stomach. You'll need to come in and do blood work, and—"

"A swollen lymph node? Hang on a minute. I need my husband to hear this as well."

Covering the phone with one hand, I opened the door, yelling, "Jim! Jim, pick up the phone!"

"Who is it?" he asked, walking down the hall.

"It's Kaiser. They found something." Eyes wide, he grabbed another phone, listening in as he paced the hallway.

"Okay, my husband is on the other line. Will you please begin again?"

"You have a swollen lymph node behind your stomach, and you'll have to do blood work tomorrow—"

"Wait, is it in my stomach or behind my stomach?"

"Well, um . . ." she hesitated.

"Is it one lymph node or two? Is there one outside and one inside?"

"Ah . . ."

"Please, just tell me what it showed."

"Oh, I wish we'd done the scan sooner!" she blurted.

Everything went cold. *Did I just hear right?*

"You need to come in tomorrow for labs. I'll place the order and you get it done. You'll probably have to go to Oahu for more testing."

"Okay."

"I'll call you in the morning and let you know what else needs to be done." And with that, she was gone.

Shaking, I stared at the dead phone in my hand. Jim wrapped his arms around me.

"You don't know what it is yet. No sense getting all worked up until we know what's going on," he soothed. "And let's wait to tell the kids."

"Yeah, but that doctor doesn't know what she's doing!" I sputtered. "What does she mean 'I wish we had done the scan sooner'? How could she say that?"

Rubbing my back, Jim said nothing. Swallowing rage, I followed him back to the dining table, pretending nothing was wrong.

"Is everything okay?" Elyse whispered.

"I just have to go for more blood work tomorrow." I answered, looking at my hands. As I tried to finish the unwanted meal, my stomach churned. Feeling as if I were watching myself in a movie, I washed the dishes, took a shower, and said good night to the kids.

Talking privately in our room late that night, I grumbled to Jim. "I can't believe that doctor. She told me I had gas and brushed me off when I told her I was afraid of lymphoma. Now she won't even give me a straight answer. I don't trust her. I'm going to email Dr. Talbot and see if he can check the scans."

"Good idea."

I went back out to our computer and pounded out a message to Dr. Talbot:

I took a CT scan today, and it showed some swollen lymph nodes. I am scared. I don't know Dr. Smithson well, and I am hoping you can either take over or give her guidance. Please look over my record and let me know what you think.

Hitting Send brought no relief. Elbows on the table in front of the keyboard, I sat resting my head in my hands. *How could this be happening? What happened to "they will find nothing"?* After a fitful, endless night, I rolled over and read "3:54" illuminated on the clock. *Close enough.* Snapping off the 5:00 alarm, I slipped out of our room, leaving Jim, snoring softly, in bed. Sitting at my desk, I clicked on my reading lamp. Sighing at my Bible, I reached past it, picking up a devotional instead. The *Our Daily Bread*[5] message for yesterday's scan day, titled "Joy in the Morning," ended with

> *New mercies every morning,*
> *Grace for each day,*
> *New hope for every trial,*
> *And courage along the way.*
> —McVeigh

God, help me.
Blowing the dust off my journal, I poured out my heavy heart to the Lord.

You told me they would find nothing . . . was it my own imaginings? It seemed so real. Jesus, you know the sorrow I feel. I have already condemned myself. Have I done anything to bring this on? Oh Lord, forgive my questioning. I have no right. No matter what happens to me, Lord, please let my family find joy in you again. Guide our steps, oh Lord.

The torrent flowed until I ran dry. Though the day was just beginning, life felt like it was ending.

---

5. Our Daily Bread, July 26, 2011, Dennis Fisher, Accessed April 25, 2017, https://odb.org/2011/07/26/joy-in-the-morning/

Later that morning at the clinic, the empty lab made for a quick blood draw. *Maybe I can speak with the doctor.* Hurrying across the hall, I stood in front of a busy receptionist sitting at her desk, headset on, fingers racing over the keyboard in front of her. I set my purse on the counter. "Excuse me, I had a call from Dr. Smithson last night, and I have some questions. Would it be possible to have a moment with her?"

Glancing at me, she held out her hand. "Let me have your Kaiser card, and I'll ask. Wait here." She disappeared through a heavy door behind her.

Several minutes later, she returned, followed by a tall nurse who reiterated that someone would get back to me soon with further instructions.

"Please, I just want to know what my CT scan said," I begged.

"You could go over to X-ray and request a copy," she offered, pointing around the corner.

"Oh, okay. Thank you."

Walking up to the X-ray department's window, I asked the young woman sitting there if I could get a copy of my CT scan results.

"I'd be happy to print that for you," she said and smiled. Handing her my medical card, she quickly typed in the request. The printer on the counter behind her whirred as the pages emerged.

"Thanks so much."

"No problem," she called over her shoulder, walking to the printer. Glancing down at the report, her smile faded. Hesitating for a moment, she looked around, as if unsure. Slowly returning to her desk, she handed the paperwork to me.

The top of the page read:

!!!ABNORMAL FINDINGS ALERT: SPECIAL ATTENTION!!!

IMPRESSION:

1. Massive abdominal and retroperitoneal adenopathy. If clinically warranted, the retroperitoneal nodes would be amenable to percutaneous biopsy.

Standing there, rereading the awful words, I mumbled, "Massive doesn't sound good." It was one of the few words I knew. That and biopsy.

"No, it doesn't," she frowned, shaking her head.

Rushing from the building, I sat outside on a concrete bench, breathing hard. *This can't be happening!* Dialing Jim's number, I felt tears slip down my cheeks. My quavering voice read the ominous words to him.

"Oh man. This doesn't sound good."

"No, it doesn't," I choked.

"Well, we just gotta wait for the doctor to get more information." He sighed, and then gently added, "I'm so sorry."

I knew he was right to wait, but I wanted answers *now*.

Feeling an unnatural heaviness, as if walking through water, I dragged myself back to the car. *Oh God, help me. I'm going to die.*

A few hours later, my cell phone rang. "Hello?"

"Hi, Eileen. Dr. Talbot here. I received your email, and I've looked over your scans. You know, it looks like lymphoma."

Lymphoma? NO! Please, God, not that! I sank into a nearby chair. *Breathe.*

"I have a few calls to make, but I'll get back to you later today," he promised.

"Okay."

Lymphoma. Just like Dad.

16

JUST LIKE DAD

Sitting on the old green love seat in our bedroom, I waited for Jim. Earlier, when I'd called him at work, sobbing about Dr. Talbot's declaration, he had promised to be right home.

Dr. Talbot called again before Jim's arrival, giving me instructions to come in the next day for another CT scan and more blood work. The day after that, I would see him to go over the test results and arrange the next steps.

In our brief conversation, he mentioned going to Oncology, but I was dazed and unable to understand what it all meant. I figured he would straighten it all out when I saw him.

Right now, I just wanted to be held. *Where is Jim?*

I also wanted to tell the kids, but Jim kept urging me to wait until we had a confirmed diagnosis.

"Maybe it's not lymphoma. Why make them worry for nothing?" he had said. While it sounded logical, it didn't seem practical.

Lymphoma.

Dad's shrunken frame filled my thoughts: hair loss after chemo, sores, swollen belly with its broken skin. *Oh Lord.*

Strangling sadness filled me. Swallowing sobs, I couldn't even form a single prayer. Jesus's name was my only thought. Jesus's name and *NOOO!*

Sounds from the living room, a TV game show, brought some small relief. At least Owen and Elyse were occupied. They wouldn't see me fall apart.

When Jim finally arrived home, he greeted the kids, then joined me in our bedroom, closing the door. Seeing him, I began to wail. I cried into his shoulder, trying to be quiet, and he rocked me until I could speak.

"Dr. Talbot wants me to do a second CT scan of my chest tomorrow. The first one only did my abdomen, but the mass is so big, he's sure it's in my lungs too."

"Oh man," Jim exhaled wiping his eyes.

"Lymphoma, Jim . . ." My voice broke.

We sat side by side in stunned silence.

"When you called me at work, I felt as if I'd been sucker punched," he whispered.

"I just feel so incredibly sad. The poor kids. I don't know what to say to them."

"But we don't know anything for sure. Best just to wait."

"Wait?" I hissed. "We have to tell the kids *something*. I can't hold this in, pretending nothing is wrong! And what about Mom and the rest of the family? I need prayer!"

Sighing, Jim bent over, holding his head in his hands. A knock on our door stopped my tirade.

"Come in," I numbly called.

Elyse led Owen into the room, her eyes mirroring the fear in my own. "What's going on?"

"Come and sit down," Jim said, standing to give her his seat. Taking his cue, I slid to the floor, patting the couch for Owen. Facing them, my resolve melted.

"My tests came back and showed some kind of swollen nodes. I'll have to go in for more testing to know for sure, but the doctor thinks it could be lymphoma."

Pacing behind me, Jim suddenly stopped, taking in a sharp breath.

"Oh Mommy!" Elyse cried. Owen grimaced as the tears began. They both knew of my father's cancer.

"I don't know what's coming, but I'll probably be sick for a while." Stroking Elyse's soft hand, I continued, "Dad will need your help around the house while I'm down. It'll be a scary time for all of us, but God will hold us."

Melding into a group hug until the first sorrow-filled wave receded, we prayed.

"God," I whispered, "We don't know what's in store. Please see us through and give us strength for the dark days ahead. In Jesus's powerful name we pray, amen."

A quiet chorus of amens followed.

Picking up the phone, I made a few calls to family members and asked for prayer. Every phone call brought gasps and tears. The news spread like wildfire, and soon folks were praying not only across the island but around the world. By evening's end, a foggy exhaustion filled my mind.

After I finally crawled into bed, thoughts of illness and death ruined my sleep. Unsure of which I feared more—the pain of illness or death itself—I tossed and turned, begging God for strength to face his plan for me.

God, I don't understand this. It makes no sense, and yet you've given this to me. Please see me through.

I'd known it was coming. Why did its confirmation hurt so?

Because it wasn't just hurting me. This hurt everyone around me. Jim, the immovable rock throughout our marriage, was shaken. And the pain on Owen's and Elyse's faces was nearly unbearable. Brandon, having just left the island, wondered if he should return. But he and I agreed that he should finish his schooling. As sad as it felt not to have him near, I knew he would come home if he needed to.

Oh God, please take away the hurt my illness is going to be on my family. Meet them where they're at and hold them.

Tossing through the night, I was haunted by memories of Dad's final months. As his strength faded, his behavior became more erratic than ever. You never knew if the help you offered would be received with a quiet "thank you" or fought with an angry "I don't need you!"

His behavior had angered me then. Now I wondered if this was my destiny.

When Dad accepted that he was dying, he turned his attention to what he could control: his funeral. He poured himself into planning every detail, calling friends to either sing a favorite hymn or to read a remembrance at the event.

"But don't say anything too good, or people will have to double-check who's in the coffin," he had joked with them.

Penning his own eulogy, Dad then sealed it in an envelope with instructions that it was to be opened only after his death by his selected emcee. When he was satisfied that everything was in place, he printed his funeral program.

As a family, we took turns sitting with him through his final days. Dad's once imposing figure shrank into a scrawny image of his former self. Still, even without mobility or speech, he maintained control with fiery glares that we dubbed "the look." Insistent visitors would see a quiet, sleeping man, but somehow, when they weren't looking, he would flash us the look, letting us know he'd had enough.

It would have been comical if it hadn't been so sad.

At Dad's funeral, though grateful for his planning, we were left empty. The humorous goodbyes for us, incorporated into his eulogy, left a hole. It felt like watching the unresolved final act of a play. Granted, he was ill while he wrote them, but it was still typical Dad style.

The longing to really *know* this man we called Dad lingered. What were his hopes and dreams? Was he satisfied with the life he'd lived? What admonishments did he have for us? What blessings for the future? Was he proud of us, his children? But none of those questions would ever be answered.

I wouldn't die that way.

Creeping out of bed before dawn the next morning, I knelt down at my old, brown chair, sobbing. "God, I want to be here. Please don't let me die. Jim is wiped out, Lord, and Brandon is so far away. Sweet Owen needs help, and you alone know Elyse's heart. Lord, I want to see the children marry and hold my grandchildren. And what about Mom? I want to care for her, Lord."

Tears fell, along with my hopes and dreams for the future.

Finally spent, I pulled myself up, sat on the chair, and cracked open my Bible to the book of Job. My hero. A righteous man, he'd lost his wealth, his children, and his health. Even his wife told him to "curse God and die." (How's that for support?) But, covered in painful boils, heartbroken, and broke, he refused, replying,

> *Naked I came from my mother's womb,*
> *And naked shall I return there.*
> *The LORD gave, and the LORD has taken away;*
> *Blessed be the name of the LORD.*
>
> —Job 1:21 (NKJV)

Wow, he blessed God.

As I leaned back in my chair, my demands for the future paled compared to thoughts of blessing God in the middle of such pain.

I much preferred God's blessing of *me*. Job's example shook my right to complain. Not knowing how to act, feel, or be with this cancer diagnosis brewing, the one thing I did know was that I wanted to leave such an example of faith for my family.

Dave Melrose, a man from my church, was one who had done just that. Dave and his wife, Nutie, had attended Waipuna Chapel for the same decades as me. The depth of love they shared with each other, their three children, and basically everyone was a beautiful thing.

Dave taught science at Maui's prestigious Seabury Hall, and Nutie shared her many talents by teaching music at the local elementary school, offering home haircuts, leading exercise classes, and even repainting bathrooms and bedrooms. Her eye for color and fun accents brightened many homes.

As their children moved into their teens, the couple became leaders for Waipuna Chapel's youth group. On weekends, Dave conspicuously parked his old beater car, dubbed the "Silver Bullet," at favorite surf spots. Teens could always find a welcome place to hang out behind the Silver Bullet.

One weekend Dave decided to try a new sport called paintball with the young men, including our oldest son, Brandon. Dressed in a thin, white T-shirt with a large, red hand-painted bullseye gracing both his front and back, Dave quickly realized he was no match for his experienced and accurate youth. Laughing about it later, he proclaimed, "Never again!"

In 2002, when their children were grown, this dynamic duo became our church's first full-time missionaries. Selling their home and most of their earthly possessions, they moved to Nicaragua where they worked with the Miskito Indians along the Rio Coco.

While there, Dave was diagnosed with cancer. It began in his gallbladder and progressed into his liver. Returning to the States, Dave and Nutie soon realized that without divine intervention he wouldn't survive.

Traveling across the mainland, Dave and Nutie visited with family and friends so he could "say all that needed to be said" before he passed away. When they returned to Maui, he continued to attend church even as his health declined, saying that worship was the only time he didn't feel pain.

Gaunt and yellowed by his failing liver, he hobbled into church his last Sunday, supported between his two sons. I watched him move to the front of the sanctuary and stand with both arms raised to heaven as the opening songs of worship began. I don't think there was a dry eye in the room as we watched his humble surrender. He died days later.

I'd never known anyone so open and honest about suffering. Dave hid nothing about pain, about shortcomings, about love. Most importantly, he shared openly about Jesus and his faith in God despite his cancer. Watching Dave's battle, I knew if I were ever to get sick like that, I wanted to be as open and brave.

If I was going to die, I wanted to die like Dave.

17

CONFIRMATION

Later that morning, I returned to Kaiser for the second CT scan. The same technician who ran the first scan helped me once again.

"Back again." I said, forcing a smile.

"How're you feeling?" he quietly asked.

"Oh, I don't know. Kind of overwhelmed, I guess. Just hoping this scan is better."

He nodded and settled me with the IV as before. The procedure mirrored the first one, thankfully without the runs.

I returned home, wondering what the next day's appointment held with Dr. Talbot. What was coming next? Would today's results be good?

Despite everything going on, I slept peacefully that night.

Once again, in that quiet, dreamy space between being asleep and awake, another vision came.

Wearing an unflattering white, sack-like gown tied at the waist, I trudged up a steep, path. Rounding a curve, I saw all the greenery of trees and bushes give way to a dusty, brown rock-strewn trail. Feeling anxious, I kept moving until I reached the top. There, I stopped.

Before me was a deep, dark crater. At its edge, I looked down between my bare feet into the valley below. The rocky path continued straight down to the crater's floor before me.

This was my destiny.

Turning left and right, I searched for a different way, but there was none. Compelled to move forward, almost as if pushed, I resisted, digging in my heels, trying to turn back. Dark shadows of things I didn't want to do, and people I didn't want to see emerged from the rolling mist below.

Panicked, holding my arms out, trying not to stumble, I cried, "No, Lord! NO! Not there! Please, NO!"

Understanding that there was no other way and I *had* to go, I stilled. My eyes followed the long pathway, across the shrouded floor of the valley, until the path started climbing up the far side of the crater's rim. As it neared the top, a breathtaking light waited.

Jesus.

"You will be healed."

Suddenly, my bedroom appeared. "Wait!" But he was gone. I looked around at this "real" world with my pulse thundering, disappointed to be back.

Staring at the ceiling, I marveled that the God of the universe, the one who holds the stars in the place, the creator of life, had come to me. To *me!* Tears slipped into my ears as I whispered, "Thank you, Jesus." *I wasn't going to die!*

My joy faded, though, as I remembered the terrible path ahead. It was true that I would see doctors I never wanted to see and do things to my body that I never wanted to do. And just what kind of healing did Jesus mean?

Wayne Watson's old song "Home Free" spoke of our ultimate healing happening when we went to heaven. Was that what Jesus meant? I'd be healed when I died? Or, would I be healed in this lifetime? Really, though, did it even matter?

Jesus said I'd be healed. He knew what lay ahead and he'd promised my healing.

"Jim," I whispered, rolling over to face him. "I saw Jesus again! He said I'd be healed!"

Jim turned toward me, silently staring. His sad eyes reflected the memory of my first dream that hadn't come true.

Carefully tucking my visions away, I rolled out of bed to prepare for the dreaded news of the day. It was Friday, July 29, and our 9:00 a.m. appointment with Dr. Talbot would give the next steps of this journey.

"This is it," I worried aloud, sitting on the exam table waiting for Dr. Talbot. Jim sighed and nodded.

Soon the doctor sailed in, grinning. "The second CT scan was *clear*. There was no sign of lymphoma in your chest or lungs." He stood nodding at the chart he held. "And that's really good news. It's so extensive in your abdomen that I was sure it had spread." The word "extensive" dampened the sense of victory.

"We need to schedule a biopsy right away, which could come back negative," he continued, "but I really don't think it will."

Still, it was a thread of hope. *Maybe it's just a weird infection.*

"I've spoken with the oncologist that you'll need to see. He's leaving for a month-long vacation next week, so I'm pushing to get everything in place before he goes." Dr. Talbot flipped through my chart. "He may have to send you to Oahu for a PET scan and maybe even the first chemotherapy treatment, but he'll talk to you about that."

Oahu? Chemotherapy?

Noticing our wide-eyed panic, Dr. Talbot paused. "You do know that this is treatable and curable, right?"

"No." I shook my head. "We didn't." *Curable! What a glorious word!*

Dr. Talbot's push made the appointments happen like rapid machine-gun fire. A lymph node biopsy was set for the following week, along with more blood work, my first oncology appointment, a bone marrow biopsy, and an echocardiogram. These tests would determine the type, stage, and treatment of the cancer.

Waiting for the testing to begin, I still made lunches for Jim each morning, and he still went to work. The kids still slept in late, enjoying the waning days of summer break. The few quiet days of life's safe monotony were passing much too quickly.

Friends called, letting us know they were praying for us. Offers of meals, house cleaning, airline mileage, and even money came in. But still feeling normal, I jokingly replied that I wasn't dying yet, and that all I really wanted was their prayers.

At church, worship music unleashed all the pent-up emotions that I didn't know how to express. Hymns like "I Surrender All," choruses of "How He Loves Us," and any song that mentioned healing left me sobbing in my seat. I seriously considered giving up mascara on Sundays. And Laura Story's song "Blessings" became my theme song.

At home, the toilet seat being left up or the toothpaste cap being left off no longer bothered me. Dirty floors and piles of laundry called for my attention but didn't present the same urgency or guilt I'd felt before.

Instead, I took up a new pastime of sitting outside, watching the clouds roll by. With pencil in hand, I journaled my frustrations, hopes, fears, and prayers, trying to sort through what was happening.

Why are such drastic measures needed, Lord, to strip us down to what really matters? Help me to trust you.

Knowing that I had no control over the future, each day's strength needed to count for something. What memories could

I make now with Owen and Elyse? With Brandon? With Jim? Notes were good. Hugs were better. Time was everything. *Give me courage, God, and please, give me time.*

August 3, clad in a thin paper gown, I waited in a cold room for the lymph node biopsy to begin. Stainless steel tables bearing sterile-wrapped packages waited with me.

Two nurses and a doctor came in, speaking in hushed voices, pulling bright lights overhead, arranging equipment, and slipping on gloves. "We're almost ready," a nurse nodded, pulling a mask over her face.

"Okay, no rush," I replied.

The doctor rolled an ultrasound probe over my abdomen, viewing the different locations of my swollen nodes. With a simple pen, he started marking my belly with an *X* on the best spots to insert the needles.

"The good thing is that your nodes are very close to the skin, so I won't have to go too deep," he stated.

Watching the ultrasound screen to my right, I asked him, "Do you think it could be an infection?"

"No, I don't think so." Placing a hand on my shoulder, he looked at me. "It has all the earmarks of lymphoma."

My heart sank, but I thanked him for his honesty. After a local anesthesia was applied, long needles drew out white fluid from two different nodes. It was done.

Admonished to rest, drink fluids, and not lift anything for a few days, I went home. Agonizing waiting commenced.

Two days later I was sitting at my desk paying bills when the phone rang. "Hello?"

"May I speak with Eileen Kusakabe?" a woman's crisp voice asked.

"Speaking." My heart started thumping erratically.

"This is Dr. Bajon. I'm a Kaiser pathologist from Oahu, and I'm calling with the results of your biopsy."

I had diffuse large B-cell non-Hodgkin's lymphoma.

Hanging up the phone, I stared at the floor. *So it's not an infection.* Guttural sobs erupted. *What do I do? Breathe. Dr. Talbot said it's curable. Jesus said I'd be healed. Breathe.*

> *What I always feared has happened to me.*
> *What I dreaded has come true.*
>
> —Job 3:25 (NLT)

I called Jim, and he came right home. We sat with Google that evening, reading all we could take in about lymphoma. There were still unknowns like "stage" and "grade," which would be determined by more testing.

As word spread to our family and friends, Kaggy called. "Do you remember last year when you did the Daniel Fast? You told me God gave you a word."

"Honestly, I don't remember, Kaggy."

"It was 'preparation,' " she reminded me.

Preparation . . . that's right. You knew all along, Lord.

18

YOU CAN'T HAVE RAINBOWS
WITHOUT RAIN

When Jim and I met Dr. Keyes, we'd never before stepped into an oncology unit. The hushed room of empty chairs and computerized IV poles was unnerving. Quietly, we followed our nurse into an exam room.

Dr. Keyes came in with a smile, introducing himself and offering quick handshakes. Sitting at the wall-mounted computer, he pulled up the image of my first CT scan.

"This is very bulky," he remarked, pointing at the white clouds filling the outline of my abdomen. "But I've seen bulkier. We'll use an R-CHOP chemotherapy, which is a series of five medications. An implanted port in your chest will save the veins in your arms, as one of the drugs can actually eat your flesh if it comes into contact with it."

Eat my flesh? Then what does it do to my insides?

"I'll send you to Oahu for the port and your first treatment. R-CHOP will break down the cancer rapidly, which is good. But, because the tumor is so large, the waste from it could compromise your kidneys. At the hospital, they can take care of any issues that may arise."

Compromise my kidneys?

"When will this all happen?"

"The sooner the better. We'll do a bone marrow biopsy tomorrow and set up a PET scan."

More awful tests. More waiting. *Ugh!*

The next day, as we sat facing Dr. Keyes in his office, he detailed the procedure for collecting bone marrow from my hip. After handing me a stack of waivers, he asked, "Any questions?"

How about we skip this one? Will this even change anything as far as my treatment is concerned? Why don't you pick on someone your own size?

"I don't think so." Sighing, I signed the forms.

Lying on my stomach in the procedure room as Dr. Keyes exposed my buttocks, I joked, "Do you need sunglasses with all that glare?"

The nurse holding my hands at the head of the table grinned.

"No, but I can use one of these freckles to mark the point of entry," he shot back.

Quickly cleaning and numbing the area, he pushed in a large needle and pulled out the red marrow. Another tool scraped off a sample of bone. When all the pushing and scraping was over, Dr. Keyes rubbed his hands together, teasing, "Okay, I just need to peel some gum from under this table to close you up, then you're free to go."

Laughing, I slowly sat up, asking, "Can you tell me anything?"

"What I *can* tell you is that your bones felt good and the marrow had a deep red color. While these are good signs, they aren't definitive," Dr. Keyes warned.

I nodded, knowing *any* cancer in my marrow would mean a stage IV rating. Still, I was encouraged. Thanking him and the assisting nurses, I limped out to where Jim waited, crying with relief.

Our next stop was picking up plane tickets and taxi vouchers for Oahu.

That weekend, we traveled off island as a family, with me checking in to Kaiser's Moanalua Hospital (MOA), and the rest of the family staying with relatives.

Sitting quietly in my sterile room early Wednesday morning, I waited. Weeks of scans, blood tests, biopsies, and finally the insertion of a hideous port in my chest the previous night, culminated in the start of chemotherapy today.

Oh God. Chemo . . .

Gingerly pressing the bandages on my chest, I felt the port, this foreign oddity that would save my veins from the poison that would save my life. Alone, watching the sun break through the misty morning, I felt warm tears rolling down my cheeks.

Outside my window, three majestic rainbow eucalyptuses—the "painted trees" I'd known since childhood—stretched to the sky. Hues of yellow, red, green, and purple peeked out from behind the wind-peeled bark of their trunks.

Aching for happier times, I remembered the grove we passed on our long, annual drives to Hana back home on Maui. Moving to the window and pressing my forehead against it, I longed to be anywhere but here.

Above the trees a small rainbow appeared in the hazy rain of the Moanalua Valley behind the hospital. God's promise.

> *I have placed my rainbow in the clouds.*
> *It is the sign of my covenant with you and*
> *with all the earth.*
> —Genesis 9:13 (NLT)

You said I'd be healed, Lord. Can't you just heal me now? Why do I have to go through this horrible chemotherapy? You're the Great Physician. Why not whisper the words, "Be healed," and take it away?

Turning from the window, I wiped my eyes on the back of my hand. A young nurse came in with my breakfast tray.

"Good morning," she said, settling it on my table. "Need anything?"

An escape plan. Shaking my head, I exhaled. "No."

"Well, let us know if you do. Enjoy." She hurried out the door.

Crawling back into bed, I perused the tray. Scrambled eggs, toast, and tea with a side of steroids, antihistamine, and Tylenol greeted me. *Will I be throwing this up later?*

I ate a few bites, then took a pill. Ate a few more bites, another pill. Finally finishing it all, I dozed until a nurse arrived with the first bag of medication.

"I'll take off that bandage and begin shortly." She nodded at my chest as she set several sterile packages on the edge of my bed. Moving fluidly from one task to the next, she washed her hands, pulled on gloves, and started opening the array of packages.

She made small talk as she worked, asking about my children and home. Pushing a large needle into my new port, she attached tubes, then bandaged and taped everything in place, and finally programmed the IV pole's monitor.

"Okay, you're all set. I'll be back to check on you soon." With one last glance at the hanging medicine bag, she was gone.

This was it. Chemotherapy.

Expecting to feel instant misery, I was surprised to feel . . . nothing. *Maybe this won't be so bad after all.*

Jim, Owen, and Elyse walked in later that morning, as the last drops of the first bag slipped into my chest. "Hi, Moomy!" Elyse smiled, giving me a big hug.

"Hi Lilu." I grinned at her use of our childhood nicknames. "How's everything in the outside world?"

"Oh, traffic's a bear," Jim grumbled, running his fingers through his hair. "I've never seen it so bad! We left later this morning, hoping to miss rush hour, but it's still awful." Weariness showed in his heavy eyes. "How's it going here?"

"I don't really feel anything yet." I shrugged.

After a watching the slow drip of IV medication and a few episodes of *Cash Cab* (a favorite for our cable-deprived family), Jim blew me a kiss as he and the kids left to find some lunch.

As the second bag finished, two nurses brought in a couple of large syringes filled with bright red liquid. This tricky medicine required so many cubic centimeters be pushed in per minute. Masked and gloved, staring at her watch, one nurse began carefully squeezing the syringe's plunger.

Watching this venomous poison slither up the tubing and into my body, I started shivering. *Poison for healing!* It made no sense, but this was war. *Do your duty, ugly poison.*

The second nurse, closely watching me, pulled a blanket up to my chin as she told me about "nadir."

"Chemo kills off fast-multiplying cells like hair, nails, intestinal cells, and the cells in your mouth," she explained. "Chemo doesn't kill adult cells, so those will hold you for about seven to ten days. Once they're depleted, there's a gap where the fast-growing cells would have been. The gap is the low point or nadir. When that hits, you'll be especially susceptible to infection."

"How long does the nadir last?"

"Only a few days. Your body will rebuild more cells in time for the next round of chemo."

The syringe, now empty, was replaced with the last bag of chemo.

After all five flavors of R-CHOP were done, exhaustion set in. My bloated abdomen protested my unwanted dinner and evening medication. As I forced down the little I could, the family walked in, brightening the evening.

Listening to their tales of driving through Jim's old college neighborhoods, seeing his favorite surf spots, and eating shaved ice, I smiled. Life went on outside.

Pulling a small package from behind her back, Elyse set it on my table with a huge grin. "What's this?"

"Open it," she said.

Travel-sized bottles of bath gel and lotion from Bath & Body Works emerged. *Warm Vanilla Sugar and White Citrus now replaced the scents of Cold Hospital Room and Off-White Bedsheet,* Elyse wrote in her new blog, UpdatesonEileen. blogspot.com. Her wit kept friends and family back home on Maui entertained and in the loop.

Our dear Maui friends, Jen and Savannah, brought real food: *manapua* (a steamed bun filled with seasoned pork), fried noodles, and Jim's favorite bitter melon dish.

Jim's sister, Claire, who lived on Oahu, visited after work, joining the buffet. By nightfall, everyone left.

"Ready to go home tomorrow?" a smiling doctor asked, looking over my chart the next morning.

"And go back to dishes and laundry?"

"Would you rather stay? If it's more comfortable for you . . ." His brow furrowed.

"No, I was just kidding. I am very ready to go home tomorrow. Thank you."

"Okay, as long as you're sure, I'll put in the discharge orders, and the nurses will give you further instructions. Take care." Patting my foot, he turned, hurrying away.

I immediately dialed Jim's cell. "We can go home tomorrow!"

"Oh, Hallelujah!"

Though the day dragged on, I couldn't stop smiling, knowing I'd soon be home.

Our discharge took longer than we'd ever imagined possible, but after a quick taxi ride, we were back at the airport that evening. With my mask and wheelchair, we breezed through TSA and quickly found our gate. Sitting there, watching the world whiz by, I felt completely ignored.

Folks scurried by, maneuvering around me as if I were a post or a piece of old luggage. If I happened to catch someone's glance, they turned away without even smiling. At first it was comical, and I laughed, purposely trying to catch people's eyes.

After a while, though, embarrassment set in, and I felt like I was back in high school, wearing fashions of the last decade.

On board the plane, Jim and I watched Honolulu's city lights fade in the distance out our little oval window. Back on Maui, Jim wheeled me down to baggage claim where our friends, Jen and Greg, picked us up. We chatted about Oahu's traffic as we drove up the Haleakala Highway in their comfortable SUV.

When we finally arrived home, our old kitchen with its stained linoleum and aging appliances had never looked so good!

When I woke Monday morning, my body ached, feeling like I had a bad flu. When I tried to stand, whiteness began to close my vision. Slipping to the floor before I passed out, I waited with my head between my knees until the room came back into view. Jim helped me shuffle to the bathroom at the speed of Tim Conway's "Oldest Man" character.

When I emerged, Jim guided me back to the old, green love seat in our room. Laying there in the fetal position, I wiped tears with the back of my hand. Jim rubbed my leg.

"Feels pretty bad, huh?"

Trying to smile, I could only offer a sad nod.

"Cup of tea?"

"Okay."

Before he left for a half day of work, Jim brought the tea, asking, "You need anything else?" *I need you to stay with me.* "No, this is fine. Thanks." With a quick kiss on my forehead, he was off.

Listening to his retreating footsteps, I heard him call, "Owen! Elyse! You're in charge until I get home."

I'm such a burden! The tears fell harder.

The kids and I muddled through Jim's daily routine of working a half day, going to the gym, and arriving home after 2:00 p.m. When he came home, he'd usually kneel beside me as I lay on the couch, give me a peck on the cheek, and then change into his yard work clothes.

"You're going outside?" I finally seethed one day.

"Yeah. Might as well do something. You need anything?"

I need you to sit and hold me!

"No," I mumbled, turning away.

After a few days of this, I opened my bleary eyes one morning to a bright, blue sky.

Yet another long day on the couch with the TV.

Staring out the window, dreading the day, I turned to see Jim readying for work.

"Morning," he said, smiling.

"Yep."

"Feeling better?"

Hmm . . . "Let me try standing up."

Jim gently helped me up. The room wasn't spinning quite as quickly as it had the day before. "I think I am feeling a bit better."

My health steadily improved, and I started sneaking chores when no one was watching. Folding the laundry as I sat in front of the TV or washing a few dishes made me happy. Imagine that! *Wanting* to do the dishes. God really *can* change hearts. My dear friend, Jen, set up a Meal Train covering two meals a week until the end of the year. (We only asked for two days a week because, in Hawaii, food is a love language. One meal usually covered us for days!) When the calendar filled, folks still called asking to bring meals between the allotted days.

This wonderful outpouring of love was hard to accept, as I preferred giving to receiving. *Is it my pride, Lord? Why is it so hard to accept help?* Pushing my feelings aside, I saw what a blessing the meals were to Jim as they gave him more time for his coping mechanism—tree removal.

Every weekend he'd be outside with either his chain saw or handsaw, cutting away an old avocado tree, branch by branch. With its roots threatening the foundation of our home, it needed to go. But he didn't stop with the tree. He then dug up, cut, and removed the huge roots, some of which were larger than my thigh!

While I understood his drive to be healthy (shoot, one of us needed to be), I wanted him to sit with me, openly sharing his thoughts, hopes, and fears about my illness. But he'd never been one to share words and emotions.

Though his silence was familiar, I ached for words. Comforting words, counseling words, love words. Day after day, he worked, exercised, and removed the tree. Night after night, he climbed into bed, barely giving me a quick kiss before rolling over and falling into an exhausted sleep.

One especially self-pity-filled night, I lay crying in bed as Jim silently rubbed my back. "Aren't you worried? I could *die!*" I wailed.

Sucking in a sharp breath, he exhaled, saying, "You shouldn't say things like that. Didn't you tell me that Jesus said you'd be healed?"

"Yes," I whispered, ashamed.

Jim was loving me as best he could. If it meant keeping busy, then so be it. My expectations of him were misplaced. No human could fill those dark, empty spaces within.

Instead, I started pouring out my nighttime anxiety to the only one who could help: Jesus. Waking often in the wee hours, with heart pounding and sweat dripping, I reminded God, "You brought me here. You promised I'd be healed. Help me through one more night. Give me a song. Hold me . . ."

My rambling requests made little sense, and I confess I was critical at times, but God lovingly answered with forgotten hymns, choruses, and eventually, sleep.

The drive down Haleakala Highway usually gave us a grand view of the velvety green West Maui Mountains surrounded by the deep blue Pacific Ocean. But this particular morning, the mountains and ocean were dark and gray, shrouded in misty rain. As the sun crested Haleakala, a stunning rainbow appeared in the haze. God's promise once again.

When we arrived at Maui's Kaiser Clinic that morning for chemo, Jim carried in the bag I'd filled with snacks, a book, and warm socks. After the first treatment in the hospital, we weren't sure what to expect on Maui.

A friendly nurse led us to a private room at the back of the unit, where an aging, overstuffed brown recliner waited with an IV pole standing behind. Beside the chair, a hospital table held a lone, silver bell.

"Make yourself comfortable," the nurse offered, waving toward the chair. "Use the bell anytime you need us."

"I need one of these at home." I grinned at Jim, fingering the bell.

"The nurse can't hear you that far away," he smirked, making me laugh.

As I settled in the recliner, Jim left for the gym, blowing me a kiss. Watching him leave, loneliness and a bit of jealousy crept in.

Treatment proceeded as before. Hours of dripping medication, a deep red push, and the uncomfortable bloating afterward.

Thus began my new life's cycle: a chemo week, a nadir week, a rebuilding week. Repeat. *God help us.*

Jim arrived when it was over with small bento lunches from TJ's. We drove to the Wailuku Community Center and parked under a shady tree to eat. A young woman, smoking a cigarette, sat on a bench nearby.

"Doesn't she know what she's doing to her body?" I grumbled. "She could wind up like me! I feel like going over there and telling her to stop it!"

"You can't do that." Jim shook his head, patting my arm.

"Well, I guess not. But why would she choose to throw away her health?" I fumed.

Glancing at the greasy food I ate, conviction hit.

Back at home, I walked around our yard for exercise, fresh air, and just to be outside. The wind, lifting the strands of my thinning hair, hurt my scalp. *Weird.*

Day after day, I'd shower, watching my hair fill the drain. Picking up the gray wad, which looked much like a wet toupee, I was sure that I must now be bald. But, I'd look in the mirror, only to be amazed that there was *still* hair on my head. Granted, there wasn't a lot of hair, and what remained could be pulled out with just a touch, but it was something.

Though only God knew the exact number of strands, chemo must have made it a whole lot easier for him to count.

Hair. I'd never given it much thought. A quick brush or blow dry was about all the attention it had gotten from me in the past. Now, I thought about it a lot. Staring at my ugly reflection as this illness transformed me, I wept.

Before nadir struck again, my friend Norma was coming for a visit. Looking around the kitchen that morning, I was happy the dishes were done, but the floor needed a sweep. *I should probably vacuum the living room, too.* But, shoot, I was sick. No one expects a clean home when you're sick. *At least this cancer is good for something!*

When Norma arrived, we chatted about our children until I brought up my hair. Or, what was left of it. "Do you think I should shave it off? I'm finding hair everywhere, and I think I'm looking like Gollum, from *Lord of the Rings*, but with better teeth."

Turning, I pointed at the sparse strands at the nape of my neck protruding from the bottom of my cap. "Do you think this works? Does it look like hair or am I just fooling myself into thinking this looks normal somehow?"

Norma answered carefully, "You do whatever makes you feel good."

An unexpected knock at the door interrupted us. "Hi!" Jen called, letting herself in. "I have a surprise for you!" Beaming, she pulled off the pink baseball cap she wore. Her long, thick, black hair was *gone!* A freshly shaved head stood in its place.

Stunned, my mouth fell open as I tried to find words. *No! Don't you know how people will look at you?* But Jen's tears through her laughter showed me love beyond reason.

"Oh my goodness!" Crying, I reached out and rubbed her GI Jane scalp. "Jen, you didn't have to do that."

"I know. I wanted to."

Norma laughed, saying, "Jen, you're so beautiful, you can totally pull off that look!"

A pair of long shiny earrings dangled where Jen's hair had been.

"From the day you told me you had cancer, I planned to do this," Jen began. "This morning, I started with a Mohawk, and

I walked around with that for a while, but it wasn't enough. So, I decided to take it all off." She told us of her three-year-old daughter, Norma Jane, who innocently asked, "Why you make your hair ugly?"

"It's not ugly. Mommy likes it. It's for Auntie Eileen."

"It's not ugly; Mommy likes it," Norma Jane had repeated, nodding her little head. Then, like a messenger on a quest, she ran through their house yelling to her siblings, "It's not ugly! Mommy likes it!"

I'm sure Norma Jane didn't understand why Mommy made her hair ugly for Auntie Eileen, but she accepted it.

If Jen could shave her head, what was I waiting for?

"It's time for me to join you. Will you do the honors?" I asked my friends.

Pulling out the clippers I used for Owen's hair, the three of us stepped into the garage. As I sat on an old, plastic lawn chair, Norma and Jen took turns gently shaving my head.

With the love of these friends, I'd get through being a shorn chemo patient.

And that night, there was no toupee in the drain.

19

HOLDING FAST TO PROMISES

Did you make your list of questions for the doctor?" Jim asked as we sat in the now-familiar oncology exam room for another follow-up.

"Yeah, I wrote out a few. Did you have anything you want to ask?"

His frisky smile and wink made me laugh. "Is that *really* all you think about?"

"No, sometimes I think about food."

Dr. Keyes walked in to our exam room with a grin. "Did you have the baby yet?"

"Very funny," I retorted.

He went on to explain that my latest CT scan showed improvement, but not eradication. "Things are progressing nicely," he reassured us. *Why can't it just be gone already?*

The next day, Jim and I set out for my third round of chemo. As we drove, a beautiful rainbow appeared to the east, over Haliimaile and Haiku.

"Huh, look at that." I pointed off to the right. "Have you noticed that whenever I go for treatment there's a rainbow?"

Jim ducked his head to see where I pointed. "No, I hadn't noticed."

Intent on the rainbow, I craned my neck, following it as long as possible. Somehow, its presence was comforting. Surely God knew what he was doing. I wasn't alone. He'd made a promise to never flood the earth again and had given Noah the rainbow as his sign to prove it. *Help me hold on to your promise, Lord.*

"What do you want for lunch today?" Jim asked, breaking into my thoughts.

"Oh, I don't know. Whatever you feel like is fine."

"Hmm . . . I guess it's TJ's again. It's close to the gym, and it's cheap."

"Yep, it is." I sighed leaning back in the seat.

Nearing the clinic, I complained, "I really don't want to do this."

"You know you have to."

"Yeah, but I'd rather go to the gym with you."

Jim squeezed my hand, but I didn't feel comforted.

Once inside, we checked in, paid, and sat outside the oncology unit, people watching. Attaching names of friends to the strangers they looked like helped pass the time. "There's Donn Anderson," Jim whispered, nodding toward an elderly haole man resembling our retired pastor.

"Uh huh," I agreed. "There's Jim Phillips," I added, glancing at a bald fellow with glasses.

Our game ended when the door opened and a nurse called my name. I took a deep breath and followed her in.

When nadir arrived this time, I noticed a loss of taste and smell, and the fuzzy thinking of "chemo fog" I had read about. Images in my mind lost their corresponding words. One rainy morning, I sat watching the deluge out our back window. "Water is overflowing . . . that thing . . ."

Jim and the kids waited quietly around the breakfast table as I fumbled for "gutter."

"It's the white thing outside . . . near the roof."

"Soffit?" Jim offered.

"No, the white plastic—"

"Flashing? Vent?" he offered, tapping his foot.

"Stop it!" I barked. "Give me a minute and I'll remember!" But his suggestions confused me, and I'd lost my train of thought. Storming to the bedroom, I burst into tears. *And I wonder why he'd rather go to the gym than be with me.*

Though we apologized later that morning, I still felt frustrated with Jim, with sickness, and with being so pathetic. My poor family never knew if I was going to bite their heads off or burst into tears. Mercifully, by week's end, my cells slowly rebuilt, and so did my emotional stability.

Driving down for the fourth round of chemo, I watched the early-morning commuters zooming around us, and I found myself envying their health. Off to the east, another spectacular rainbow followed us for several miles. *Thank you, Lord. I hate this, but you're still here. Please see me through today.*

When we parked at Kaiser, I didn't move. Jim squeezed my knee. "Come on. You can do it!"

"Do I have to?"

"Yep. Doctors' orders." He smiled, but in his tired eyes I saw sorrow.

Sitting outside the oncology unit, I stared at its heavy door. It was made of plain brown wood with a slender, vertical window that had been papered over, leaving only a small slit to peek through. A secret society that no one wanted to be part of. Including me.

The door opened. "Eileen? Ready for you."

Before nadir hit, I ventured outside to warm myself on a beautiful sunny morning. As I sat on a new lounger, the clear day gave a spectacular view of Haleakala's summit. The brightness of the morning prompted me to close my eyes and talk with God.

Earlier that morning, I'd read in my *Streams in the Desert*[6] devotional about how a bar of steel's value increased through merciless hammering, firing, and polishing. A $5 bar could eventually become $250,000 worth of springs for watches.

Is that what this is about, Lord? Are you working me to make me more valuable?

I don't understand all of this, Lord. I feel your love through people's prayers and in the many hands that help us, but I'm worried about the future. Are you going to heal me here on earth?

Tears fell as a deep calmness settled. God held me even when I didn't trust.

Thank you, God, that I can be honest with you. I'll wait as you work on me. I know you'll see me through this season.

Maybe this wasn't just about me, my family, my friends, or my church. Maybe it was just a tiny part of a bigger scheme—a tiny mosaic piece in the beautiful landscape of God's universe. Maybe cancer was merely a tool, chiseling away rough edges.

Marveling that God could use *anything*—even cancer—to complete his handiwork, I felt a strange feeling of worth, acceptance, and value crept in. God had chosen this path, he was working in me, and he loved me. Completely.

---

6. L. B. Cowman, "October 24," *Streams in the Desert*, Christianity.com, accessed April 25, 2017, http://www.christianity.com/devotionals/streams-in-the-desert/streams-in-the-desert-october-24th.html.

A few days later, nadir's vengeance dissolved any sense of worth. Hiding in my room, with no way around the misery, I spent my days of horizontal life watching reruns of *The Waltons* and *Who Wants to be a Millionaire?*

As bad as the days were, the nights were worse. Listening to Jim's deep, steady breaths, my mind couldn't stop worrying: *What if I have to do eight treatments? Will chemo take care of the cancer? What if I need a stem cell transplant? Will I die?*

As I begged God for rest, an old song by the band 4Him called "Where There Is Faith" sang of "a peace like a child sleeping." The previously forgotten melody soothed my fears until I dozed off. I clung to the ballad for many long nights.

Preparing for my next CT scan, I talked with my nephew's wife, Crystal, telling her I hoped to end chemo soon. Crystal told me that her friend, who worked at the Mayo Clinic, said to take *all* cancer treatment offered. "If you're offered chemo or radiation, do them both. It's *that* important to make sure the cancer is killed."

Not what I wanted to hear.

When the scan was complete, the technician showed me the images.

"Looks like the cancer is still reducing. Chemo is doing its job." He turned to me offering a thumbs-up.

"So it's still there," I whispered, trying to mask my disappointment. I'd have to do more chemo.

The next morning, while I read the *Our Daily Bread* devotional, words leapt off the page: "What is your worst fear? If you should have to face it, Christ will be there with you. Trusting him through prayer makes available 'the peace of God, which surpasses all understanding.' "

My current worst fear was more chemo. *But more chemo isn't nearly as scary as the chemo not working.*

Opening the Bible to Hebrews chapter 5, I read that Jesus learned obedience through suffering. *Jesus needed to learn obedience?*

Though I liked to think that I was obedient, God knew the truth. *Shoot, if even Jesus learned through his suffering, surely I can trust and learn, too.*

Jim met me for my appointment with Dr. Keyes to get the results of my last scan. Though I knew in my heart that I would need all eight treatments, I didn't want the confirmation. Waiting in the exam room, Jim took my hand. "It'll be okay. We'll get through this."

Dr. Keyes came in, saying my scan looked great. Pulling it up on his computer monitor, he stared at it for a few moments and then pulled a small ruler from his pocket. Measuring some of the gray dots, he turned to Jim and me.

"You know, you might be able to finish with just two more treatments, but I'd like to look at the scans with the radiologist. I don't want to miss anything. Would you mind waiting?"

"Of course not," I replied.

When he returned, he confirmed my fear. "You still have a few enlarged lymph nodes. Normal nodes are less than 1.0 centimeter, but a couple of yours are still about 1.7 cm."

I looked at the ceiling, willing the tears to stop.

"We *could* stop treatment after the sixth round," he explained, "but if there's any active lymphoma left, you'd have to go for a stem cell transplant at that point."

Thinking back on my conversation with Crystal, I replied, "Let's go for it. I don't want any regrets for stopping early."

"You're sure?"

"Yes." This decision meant I was only halfway through treatment.

As we drove for the next round, I began my "I don't want to do this anymore" mantra. Jim let me moan all I wanted, and when I stopped, he quietly reminded me, "You have to do it." *Sigh.*

I looked for my rainbow, and sure enough, one hovered over Haliimaile.

Oh Lord, thank you. I hate this, but your promise is true.

At Kaiser, the now-familiar faces at the reception counter warmly greeted me, asking with genuine concern, "How are you doing?"

Well, do you want to hear about my sleepless nights? Anxiety? Frustration? Or how about a long dissertation on my bowel function? How much time do you have?

"I'm fine, but could be better," I'd say.

Back to the familiar stuffed chair and the squeaky IV pole. Back to the TV and the cold. Jim left for the gym, and I snoozed between bathroom breaks, beeping machines, and new chemo bags. Before I knew it, it was over.

Jim returned, and we dined on bentos in the shade at Kahului Shopping Center for a change of scenery. Even though I had dozed all morning, I was tired. Chemo was getting harder.

At home, I flopped on our bed. I was tired. So tired. Turning on the TV, I hoped to turn off my brain. Round five was finished, and nadir lurked around the corner.

My chemo fog was more pronounced now. Not only did I forget words, midsentence I'd completely forget what I was talking about. My vision worsened, as well as my hearing, and even my sense of touch. My fingers felt as if they were coated in dried glue.

Nadir came and left, and by the following week I felt somewhat normal again. Thanksgiving fell during that "good" week. Jen's family graciously hosted us, along with many other friends. I sat like a queen on their sofa, wrapped in a warm, fuzzy blanket.

"For you," Jen said, bending down to hand me a plate loaded with turkey, mashed potatoes, and stuffing, all covered in gravy. Chow mein, a green-bean casserole, and cranberry sauce rounded off the plate, with a pumpkin square set aside for dessert.

"Mmm . . . it looks so good!"

"Just let me know what else you need," she grinned.

"Probably a nap if I finish it all."

"You know where my room is."

Family and friends around me chatted about football and the weather. Reclining, watching loved ones enjoying one another, listening to their banter, I thanked God for the day. Mostly, I savored this first Thanksgiving since childhood where I didn't have to wash dishes. What a gift!

20

FINISHING WEAK

Christmas was just around the corner and there were jellies to be made, cookies to be baked, and cards to be mailed. Our Christmas tree was up, and a few gifts were on the way, thanks to Amazon. Shopping online in my pajamas, I hurried to finish all I could on my good days.

Staring out the car window as we drove down for round six, I imagined skipping treatment and hitting the beach. Warm sand, lapping waves, floating in the ocean . . . though, to be honest, even a day at the dump would be a welcome change from chemo.

I twisted in my seat, looking for my rainbow. A small, faint one frowned off in the distance over Haiku.

"Can't get comfortable?" Jim glanced at me with a furrowed brow.

"Nah, I'm fine. I just don't want to go."

He rolled his eyes at my familiar complaint.

Nadir arrived a week later. Lying on the couch, my eyes searched our Christmas tree, as I marveled at our family's many picture ornaments. *Wow, I was healthy then . . . and I had hair!*

Health, so exotic and far away, seemed a just-out-of-grasp fantasy or a dreamlike memory. This season of slowing down, resting, and worst of all, relying on others felt . . . wrong. Un-American even. But my wonderful family kept going when I couldn't.

December brought Christmas joy and laughter. Friends continued bringing food and our longtime friend Sue brought along a funny Christmas hat with her dinner. Though shaped like a Santa hat, it sported working Christmas lights around the brim and played "Holly, Jolly Christmas." The jingle bell on the pointed top swung back and forth to the rhythm, hitting me in the head. I wore it as long as I could stand it, and we both howled in laughter.

"Do you think I could wear this to the candle-lighting service on Christmas Eve?" I yelled over the cacophony.

"Absolutely! You can get away with anything."

As my next CT scan date approached, my anxiety peaked. The possibility of going to California for a stem cell transplant became more real if this one wasn't clear. Reading online about the dreaded procedure only worsened my fear.

Oh Lord, you said I would be healed. How far do I have to go for healing?

In a perfect world, one would achieve remission and then do two more rounds of chemo to finish off any hidden cancer cells. But I hadn't yet reached remission. With only two more rounds of R-CHOP available to me, I needed to be in remission *now*.

The morning of the scan, I sat in the cold reception area with several other people waiting for scans and X-rays. Holding up my barium, I joked with a woman nearby, "Want a swig?"

Grinning, she shook her head. "Thanks, but I have my own."

I caught the eye of the woman next to her, who frowned at me and shook her head before turning away. Embarrassed, I quickly finished the drink and hurried down the corridor. Feeling chilled in both body and spirit, I walked outside in the bright sunshine until the barium settled. Palm trees swayed in a gentle breeze as two mynah birds hopped along the hot asphalt.

Oh Lord, this is it. Please let this be the scan where "they will find nothing."

Early the next morning, Jim and I lay in the still darkness talking over the events of the past months. "This has been one of the hardest things I've ever done," I whispered. "And I know it's been hard on you, too."

"Yeah," Jim replied. "But you're almost there. Almost done."

"I'm praying I'm in remission, but what if I'm not?"

"You gotta try not to think about all the bad things. You still have two more treatments to do, and that could do it."

He's right. I can't focus on the bad.

Later that morning, at Kaiser once again, we waited for the results of my scan. Dr. Keyes opened the exam room door. "How's it going?"

"That's what we're waiting to hear," I said.

Taking out his ruler, Dr. Keyes held it against the image on his computer screen for a quick measurement. "Well, there is continued improvement with more reduction in one of the nodes." He leaned back, folding his arms across his chest.

"That's a good thing, right?"

"Yes, but since the cancer is still reducing, it means it's still active. The chemo is still working, though it's not working as quickly as before."

The cancer is still active.

"So I'm not in remission?"

"Not yet, but you are *really* close." He held his thumb and forefinger close together in front of his eyes.

"So, after I finish chemo, I go for the PET scan. If the PET scan shows cancer, it's the stem cell transplant, right?"

Dr. Keyes paused, taking a deep breath before answering. Looking at me over the top of his glasses, he said, "While that's true, I'm confident that the next two rounds will put you into remission. Remember where you started." Turning back to his computer, he pulled up the original scan next to the latest scan. "It's really quite remarkable how far you've come."

"You're right," I admitted, looking at the tiny dots of cancer that were once huge clouds. *But I wanted remission today.*

Jim squeezed my shoulders. "Good thing we decided to go for all eight treatments. Thank you, Dr. Keyes, for your good advice."

At dawn on the morning of December 17, Brandon arrived home for Christmas. His energy and easygoing style livened up our tired home. Over the week that he was back, we saw *Sherlock Holmes* at the theater and drove to Ulupalakua's wine-tasting room for samples. He took Owen and Elyse to the beach one day and set up his Xbox Kinect for dance competitions in the evenings. Brandon won often, but Elyse learned quickly and soon challenged him. Jim and I attempted the moves and laughed our way through. The days of activity blurred into a happy mess.

One morning, Brandon bounded into the kitchen. "It's been so intense at school, Ma. But here I'm finally feeling like I can breathe again. It's so good to just relax! No school, no tests—just rest and free food!"

Turning from the sink where I'd been washing dishes, I laughed. "I'm so glad you're here, B. And I'm really proud of you."

"Thanks, Mama!" He hugged me tightly adding, "I'm proud of you too."

"Aww, thanks, B."

Pulling back, he took a deep breath. "Maybe I don't worry about you as much as I should, but I know you're going to be fine. I don't know how or why, but I just know."

"Well, that's encouraging. But I still expect some pity every now and then. And a phone call once in a while."

"Okay, Mama." He laughed, rolling his sparkling brown eyes.

On Wednesday the 21st, I completed my seventh round of chemo. The morning rainbow was the only bright spot in the day of pills, drips, syringes, and boredom. Then a tasteless lunch and a tiring drive home. Fatigue, insomnia, discouragement, and uncertainty followed suit. It was enough to make a grown woman cry. The one consolation was that Christmas would come before nadir. Thank God for small miracles.

Jim's sister, Claire, arrived on Christmas Eve. We hadn't seen each other since the hospital in August. We shared tears as we hugged and she reminded me that this illness was only temporary.

At home that evening, we relaxed, sipping some Ulupalakua wine under Christmas tree lights. My overloaded kidneys kept me at only one sip, and Owen and Elyse joined us with sparkling cider.

"I'm so glad we're all together," I said, looking at each one.

"Toast!" Brandon called. "Here's to family and being together."

Clinking our glasses and hugging, we then talked late into the night.

Christmas arrived on a crisp and clear Sunday morning. The blur of eating a hearty breakfast, opening gifts, attending a short church service, and gathering with our extended family granted us a reprieve from chemo and illness.

When we returned home that evening, Brandon packed for his flight the next day. Claire stayed a few more days, cleaning everything in sight, and earning the nickname "Alice," like the housekeeper in the *Brady Bunch*.

Expecting nadir to leave me flat by Tuesday or Wednesday, I was pleasantly surprised to still be standing on Thursday. *This is great! Maybe I'll skip nadir altogether.*

But, Friday morning, I was sitting at the breakfast table when galaxies of stars started swirling in my head. Sliding to the floor, I lay down next to the wall, panting like a dog, trying to stay conscious.

The initial wave passed, and Jim helped me hobble back to the bedroom. Back to the green couch. Back to isolation. *I hate this! I don't want to do it anymore! I quit!*

Strangely, though, nadir didn't last long. By that same afternoon, I could walk down the hall without fainting.

Three times that week, I received notes of encouragement that included the same verse:

> *But those who trust in the LORD will find new strength.*
> *They will soar high on wings like eagles.*
> *They will run and not grow weary.*
> *They will walk and not faint.*
> —Isaiah 40:31 (NLT)

I wanted to walk and not faint. I needed new strength. *Would I remember to trust?*

By January 5, we were post-holiday, the Christmas tree gone and decorations put away. Life resumed its routine, with Elyse struggling to catch up on her schoolwork, Owen preparing for his next semester at college, and Jim back at work. Feeling like a human being again, I made dinner that night.

The next morning at breakfast, Jim thanked me for making dinner. He then proceeded to thank me for taking down the Christmas tree, tidying the house, and making his breakfast and lunch.

It was nice to be thanked for doing the ordinary chores I'd been unable to do for so long.

Later, I emailed a thank you to him for going to work and providing for the family. I laughed when he emailed back and thanked me for thanking him.

Thankfulness was a good thing. I needed to practice it more. It was a much better default than the worry and self-pity I'd been perfecting.

Lord, have I thanked you for your provision of life, breath, food, shelter, health? The salvation of my soul?

Tuesday morning, I wakened with a runny nose. As the morning progressed, so did my tissue usage. Picking up the phone, I dialed Oncology. "Hi, this is Eileen Kusakabe. I'm set for my last chemo treatment tomorrow, but I have a runny nose. Can I still do it?"

"Do you have a fever?" the nurse asked.

"No, no fever."

"How badly do you feel?"

I thought about it a moment before answering. "Just tired, but I'm always tired."

"You should be all right," she stated, "as long as you don't have a fever or feel flu-like symptoms."

"Shucks," I joked. "I was trying to call in sick!"

"Nice try."

That evening, packing my bag for the last time, I curiously felt anxious about ending treatment. *How many times have I groaned to Jim that I don't want to go, and now I don't want it to end? Weird.*

As much as I wanted chemo done, I wanted this cancer *gone.* Would it be enough? I'd have to wait six weeks to do the PET scan to make sure all the chemo had cleared my system and didn't skew the test. Six long weeks.

Shaking my head, I scolded myself. *Focus!* First things first. Get through the last round of chemo.

The next morning, heading down to the clinic with Jim, I didn't have to look for my rainbow. The misty morning gave way to a stunning one hovering over the road in front of us. But its brightness didn't break my gloom. With my head against the headrest, I closed my eyes as the tears fell. *I am so, so tired of this.*

Glancing at me, Jim pushed my shoulder. "Hey, cheer up. Last one today!"

Looking at him, I said nothing. I couldn't even smile.

Keeping one hand on the steering wheel, he rubbed my arm with the other.

Staring out the windshield, I whispered, "Yeah, I know. I should be happy, but I hate this."

"You got this. You can do it."

Easy for you to say.

"Hey, what about lunch today? We should do something special!" He skillfully changed the subject. "I know—we could go to a *real* restaurant instead of eating bento in the car." Smiling, he wiggled his eyebrows up and down.

I couldn't resist his enthusiasm and smiled back. "Always about the food."

"You know it!" he chuckled. "Hey, we could go to Matsu."

"That's only because you like the deep-fried akule!" The tropical fish, also known as big-eyed scad, was one of Jim's favorites.

"Well, you can't taste anyway," he countered. "I might as well get something *I* like."

Shaking my head, I laughed. "True . . . okay, let's go to Matsu afterwards. You win."

He raised his fist in triumph.

During treatment, on one of my trips to the restroom, I saw our friend Daryl and his wife, Deena, in the room next to mine. Daryl was fighting terminal cancer and beating unbelievable odds. But today, he didn't look well. His weakened frame slouched in his plush chair beneath a mound of blankets. Deena sat on the edge of a plastic chair watching Dr. Keyes and a nurse attend to him.

Oh Lord, please cover Daryl. He has been fighting for so long. His family needs him, Lord!

Back in my room, waiting to be done, I cried for Daryl.

God, you could heal him with one word! Daryl should be having his last treatment. His children are so young. God, this isn't fair! It's not right!

But nothing changed.

Jim arrived shortly afterward, and I was done. *I was done!*

Dr. Keyes stuck his head in the doorway, "Seems like you were just here three weeks ago!"

"Ha ha. Very funny." I shook my head with a smile.

Before he walked away, the nurse removing my IV commented, "This is her last treatment."

"Is that right?" Dr. Keyes looked back at me.

"Yep, and I even have some fuzz up here to prove it." Pulling off my hat, I rubbed my stubbly head.

"That's just secondary hair. It'll fall out too," he said, totally bursting my bubble.

"Secondary hair? Does everyone have that?" Jim asked.

Dr. Keyes rubbed his follicly challenged head and smiled. "Nope." We all laughed. I loved my doctor.

Picking up my belongings, I looked around, gazing at the room for the last time. I'd miss the good people here. As I followed my nurse out of the room, she gushed to another nearby nurse, "She's all done today. She's a graduate!"

"Oh, congratulations!"

Be quiet! Daryl and Deena can hear!

Grimacing, I whispered, "Thank you," and cast a glance at Daryl's room. The nurses caught the motion and quieted.

We looked in on Daryl and Deena before we left. Daryl turned to face us, weakly lifting his hand in greeting. His shallow breathing and ashen face exposed his pain. "Congratulations," Deena whispered through tear-rimmed eyes. My heart shattered.

Walking to the car, I murmured to Jim, "I don't think Daryl is going to make it."

"He didn't look too well, did he?"

"No, he looked pretty bad."

Silently, we drove to Restaurant Matsu where Jim ordered his deep-fried fish. The small establishment offered few tables, and all were occupied. Hovering for a few minutes until someone stood to leave, I quickly took their spot. Jim cleared and wiped the table.

"Whose idea was this anyway?" he winked.

The food arrived quickly, and we prayed a blessing on both the food and Daryl. When our meal was done, we stepped outside into brilliant sunshine. It was the beginning of a new chapter.

21

LATER, NADIR

A week after the final round of chemo, the nadir was noticeably mild. No longer seeing oceans of stars as I walked through the house, I wondered if the medicine was no longer working. Regardless of what the chemo did or didn't do, I was *done* with it. Done with nadir. And hopefully done with cancer.

The six-week wait before the PET scan gave me much time to contemplate where I had been, who I was now, and what the future held. While my most pressing questions were about further treatment, I couldn't help but dream that I was done. *What happens when you're done with cancer? What do people do with this second chance at life? Travel? Shop? Get a tattoo of the word cancer with a big, red, circle-backslash symbol over it?*

Though I wanted answers and longed to celebrate, I had to wait.

Life took on a blur of normal-ish activity. Owen continued school at the University of Hawaii Maui College and volunteered with Hawaii Canines for Independence, while Elyse struggled to finish her junior year of online high school. Jim

179

worked and went to the gym, and I washed dishes and laundry, bought groceries, and paid the bills.

Without a date for the definitive test, I decided to busy myself with painting our dingy living room. At The Home Depot, I picked out a nice tan color called "Warm Muffin." As I began the first wall, Owen walked by, asking, "You're painting the living room orange?"

It was true. The color wasn't a nice tan. It looked more like the combination of mustard, ketchup, and mayonnaise that we used to get at Dairy Queen for our french fries.

"No, it's 'Warm Muffin.' "

At my next oncology appointment, I expected to be given my PET scan date. The appointment quickly became a disappointment.

"The request for your PET scan will be put in today," nurse practitioner Amy explained. "Once it's approved, you'll receive a call to make your appointment. When that's set, contact the travel department here, and they'll arrange your flights and taxi vouchers."

More waiting. *There's got to be a better way of doing things.*

The next day, I received an email requesting prayer for Daryl. He was home under hospice care. *Oh Lord . . .*

Daryl's upbeat countenance over his long battle was phenomenal. With an initial diagnosis giving him only weeks to live, he battled on and was still living more than two years later. Despite the pain and exhaustion of his journey, his eyes still flickered with mischievousness.

Months before, Daryl and his adoring wife sat in Waipuna Chapel, near the front on the left-hand side. Pastor Dale stood behind the pulpit, preaching from the Old Testament book of Ecclesiastes on Solomon's quest for life's meaning.

Filling a large bowl with Lay's potato chips as he spoke, he recounted the company's slogan, "You can't eat just one."

"It's not because Lay's are better than everything else. It actually says more about us than the Lay's. There is something inside of us that keeps wanting . . . one . . . more." With that, he picked up a crispy chip and crunched it in his mouth.

Dale offered the bowl to a few hesitant parishioners, but no one ventured to accept it. He shrugged, sampled another chip, and then set the bowl aside. (To his credit, he also offered carrots for those who were more health conscious.)

As Dale continued the sermon, Daryl suddenly stood up, strode to the stage, passing right in front of Dale, and picked up the bowl of chips. Pastor Dale stopped midsentence, whispering a bit too loudly, "What are you doing?"

"Can't let these go to waste," Daryl smiled. The congregation erupted in laughter and applause. As Daryl strolled back to his seat, he took a few chips and then passed the bowl to those around him. Eventually, it worked its way up and down each row of the church.

A red-faced Pastor Dale shook his head, grinning from ear to ear. "I did *not* ask him to do that!"

Daryl passed away on February 21. He was just forty-one years old.

His passing sparked a profound, hollow sadness within me. How much more so for his family and friends. Cancer was an ugly, ugly thing. *How do I feel grateful for something that opened my eyes to you, God, but robbed this beautiful family of their father? Their son? Her husband?* It made no sense whatsoever.

> "For my thoughts are not your thoughts, neither are your
> ways my ways,"
> declares the LORD.
> "As the heavens are higher than the earth, so are my ways
> higher than your ways
> and my thoughts than your thoughts."
> —Isaiah 55:8-9 (NIV)

God, I know your ways are higher, but why Daryl? Why now?
No answers came.

All throughout this season, I'd turned to my biblical hero Job for help. Opening my Bible again, I read through his righteous striving to please God. *Yep, I can relate to that.*

But God still allowed him to suffer tremendously through losing his wealth, his children, and finally his health.

Oh God, why? How could you do that to someone so upright?

The story continued with Job's friends coming for a visit. At first, they sat silently grieving with him for an entire week. Maybe they even shaved their heads for him, like Jen did for me.

Unfortunately, they then opened their mouths: "What sin did you commit to deserve this? Must have been pretty bad" (Eileen Abridged Version).

Well-intentioned people had asked me questions about my diet and what had caused my cancer. How many times I'd wanted to retaliate with "I exercise too much" or "I ate too many vegetables."

Why do we do that, Lord? Why do we expect nice, tidy answers to life's tragedies?

Job insisted on his innocence, but no one believed him. Society spurned him, his wife withdrew, his body decayed, and he finally gave up, declaring it would have been better to die at birth than to bear God's unjust wrath.

> *Now summon me, and I will answer!*
> *Or let me speak to you, and you reply.*
> *Tell me, what have I done wrong?*
> *Show me my rebellion and my sin.*
> —Job 13:22-23 (NLT)

It sounded to me like Job was saying, "If only God would give me five minutes of his time. I've got some serious problems with this plan he's mapped out for me."

God's answer to Job's request is recorded in the four long, unrepentant chapters of Job 38-41. But, instead of an inspiring explanation of all that's happening, God gives Job the smack down.

> *Who is this that questions my wisdom*
> *with such ignorant words?*
> *Brace yourself like a man,*
> *because I have some questions for you,*
> *and you must answer them.*
>
> *Where were you when I laid the foundations*
> *of the earth?*
> *Tell me if you know so much.*
>
> —Job 38:2-4 (NLT)

Unrelenting, God questions Job's wisdom on everything from directing the movement of the stars, to making a hawk stretch its wings and soar. Over and over God points out his supreme wisdom and might as it is displayed in all of creation.

Oh man, God. He just wanted to know why this was happening after he'd tried so hard to serve you. Aren't you being too harsh? I'd be crushed if you dealt with me like that.

Job must have been crushed too. The Bible says he covered his mouth in shame, acknowledging that "you can do anything, and no one can stop you" (Job 42:2 NLT).

Oh Lord, was I wrong to ask how to know you? Am I incapable of recognizing your power and wisdom? God help me. Help me to see. Keep me from doubting you.

For all the many times I'd read Job, I'd never felt his pain as clearly as I did now. And yet I knew my suffering was part of God's plan for me. Job never knew what hit him.

At the end of Job's story, the humbled man prayed for his judgmental friends, and God blessed him with more children, more wealth than he'd had before, and another 140 years of life.

But what about his first children? Did the ache of loss ever go away?

I don't think it did.

Job submitted. Jesus submitted. Even after reading God's proclamations of his greatness, I struggled to submit to an authority I couldn't understand.

While I understood that submission to authority was required with loathsome taxes and high gas prices, submitting here felt hopeless. I could always find deductions for my taxes or change my withholdings so they didn't hurt so much. And gas prices fluctuated like the wind. They'd go down eventually.

But I was powerless to change anything with Daryl's outcome. Though many prayed for Daryl's healing, he still died. His time on this earth was done.

Time progressed toward the defining scan date. I waited, worried, and prayed. As much as I longed to know if I was in remission, the fear of *not* being in remission sickened me. With the future on hold, I tried to relax and enjoy whatever time I had left.

But to relax meant to be still and quiet. Precious quiet time brought deep questions. Usually in the middle of the night.

On one of those long, sleepless nights, I lay in bed pondering remission. *Remission . . .* did I dare to hope? Or would I wind up disappointed?

And if I was truly in remission, what would life look like? Would it simply revert to homeschooling and chores? Or was it time to get a job? What about all the lessons learned? Would I forget? I hoped not. I wanted to be forever altered. I wanted to stay "real."

But what was real? Work, chores, email, bills—was that it? Maybe throw in a vacation here and there? After this experience, that life seemed hollow.

As much as I hated being stripped of my hair and health, it brought down pretension and fostered openness with those around me. Friends and strangers asked about my cancer and spoke openly of their experiences with the dreaded disease. Whether they had been through it themselves or watched a loved one with it, there was solidarity in suffering.

This camaraderie of vulnerability was real.

Is this what you want, Lord? Me to be real with you? Vulnerable? Able to recognize my own limitations and your limitless power?

Peace warmed me like a thick blanket on a chilly night. I didn't have the right words. I didn't pray the right prayers. It was okay to question what I didn't understand. My thoughts didn't change who God was. And God loved me regardless of what I felt or believed.

But not just me. He loved *everyone* this way.

Lord, whatever you have for me to do, I want to do for you. I want to live for you. To proclaim that you are real, that you love us beyond measure. That bad things are opportunities for you to reveal yourself to us, even when we don't understand.

God had a plan, and he would fulfill his purpose in my life. I drifted back to sleep.

22

TRUSTING AND LEARNING

To celebrate the end of chemo, Jen gifted me with a massage from our dear friend and amazing masseuse, Sue. Lying on my stomach in her studio, as she gently rubbed my back, she asked, "Is there anywhere that you want me to focus on?"

"Not really. I find that my joints are pretty sore, though. I've been trying to exercise a bit, and it makes me hurt."

Sue stopped and jokingly scolded, "Can I remind you that your body has been through a lot? REST. Give it time to recover before you try and get back into exercise." She worked on my shoulders and pressed alongside the vertebrae of my back. "Boy, your skin is just drinking up all the oil I keep putting on."

"Yeah, I've noticed it's pretty dry. I guess you'll have to charge Jen extra for all the oil."

Sue laughed and kept pouring on more oil.

Her hands felt wonderful on my shoulders and back. The cool room and peaceful music lulled me to sleep. Before I knew it, it was done. Sue tapped my leg to waken me.

"All finished," she whispered.

"Oh, that was wonderful," I purred.

"Let me pray with you before you go." She placed her hand on my shoulder. "Lord, please cover my sister and watch over the scan results. Bless and keep her, and Jim, and the kids too. We love you, Lord, and we trust you with the future. Amen."

The peace that flowed from her simple prayer was as powerful as the relaxation that flowed from her hands. I floated back to my car and drove home for a nice long nap.

On March 1, Jim and I flew to Oahu for the PET scan. We woke early and set out for our 9 a.m. flight, with our return to Maui scheduled for later that evening.

"This is it," I whispered, standing in line at the security checkpoint. Jim rubbed my back and squeezed my shoulders.

"It'll be fine," he assured me. "Remember, Dr. Keyes was sure that the last two rounds of chemo would put you in remission."

"You're right. It's just hard to keep those ugly thoughts away."

Before long, we arrived on Oahu and were whisked by taxi to the lab. We arrived in plenty of time for the 11:30 a.m. appointment and decided to wait outside in the warm sunshine. Jim ordered a coffee at a neighboring store, and we sat at a table under a bright red umbrella.

"Still worried?" Jim asked.

"Yeah. Pray for me."

Jim reached over, taking my hand. "God, please let this be quick and easy for Eileen. Please give us a clear result. Amen."

"Thank you, honey. It means a lot to me." Tears threatened, but I brushed them away.

Before long, I was called in and the test was repeated as before treatment. IV drip, lie still for half an hour, a shot of contrast, scan for forty-five minutes, then freedom.

"How long will it be before my doctor receives the results?"
I stopped to ask the receptionist on our way out.

"He should have the results tomorrow."

Tomorrow.

Jim's Uncle Jiggs picked us up and drove us to his home
in Pauoa Valley. We sat on their covered *lanai* (porch), gazing
up at his beautiful garden poised on the steep hill behind his
home. Sparrows and mejiro (Japanese white-eye birds) flitted
about the trees and rocks. Jim asked about the care of such
a large garden and the difficulty of the terrain. Uncle Jiggs
smiled, saying he just took it slow.

The peaceful setting belied my inner turmoil.

Claire joined us after work, and then drove us back to the
airport for our return flight to Maui.

The next day I waited for a phone call from Dr. Keyes but
heard nothing. I refused to call. If bad news was coming, I
wanted to delay the outcome for as long as possible.

Good or bad, I'd know soon enough with my next oncology appointment.

Surely they would call if it was good news.

On March 3, we attended Daryl's funeral. Pastor Dale
flew in from California (where he and his family had recently
relocated) to officiate the funeral. Ballard Funeral Home
overflowed with hundreds of mourners. We joined the long
procession and hugged Deena, Daryl's parents, and his sisters.

Dale shared funny memories of his friendship with Daryl,
including the potato chip heist. Dale went on to explain the
serious side of their friendship and how Daryl had accepted
Jesus as his Savior. The comfort and hope of heaven encouraged all.

As we drove home, the reality poured over me like a bucket
of iced water. People died from cancer.

I could die from cancer.

All those months of treatment, I held tightly to my Jesus
dreams. But now the reality of death played out in front of

me. A sorrow-filled widow, fatherless children, grieving parents. *Why did God allow suffering and death? It shouldn't be so!*

For several days, the darkness of doubt, hurt, and guilt over Daryl's untimely death, kept me tossing through the night and exhausted each morning.

And yet, God was still good. The Bible said so. I had seen Jesus. I had felt his peace. I knew it was so.

I want to trust you, Lord, even though I don't understand. You love Deena and her children more than I am capable . . . and yet you let Daryl die. You allowed it. Help me to trust you for them and remember to pray for them. Provide the comfort they need, oh Lord.

Though I resolved to trust God and believe he was good, the dark sorrow remained.

The night before my oncology visit and pending scan results, Jim and I attended a small group Bible study at a friend's house. While there, Jim asked the group to pray not only for a good outcome but for peace. Encircling us as we stood, our friends held our shoulders, bowed their heads, and prayed aloud.

The deep darkness fell away.

Back at home that night, I slept peacefully for the first time since Daryl's funeral.

The next morning, Jim drove me down to Oncology for the PET scan results. Grabbing his hand as we entered the clinic, I held on tightly, even in the exam room.

"It's going to be okay," he said, rubbing my hand with his thumb.

Dr. Keyes walked in, saying, "I guess you've heard already?"

"No, I never called. What's the news?"

Dr. Keyes held up an official-looking report. "Full remission!"

"Oh, thank you, Jesus!" I threw my arms around Jim.

"Wonderful news." Jim exhaled into my neck. Pulling away, I reached for a tissue on the counter behind me. Jim, wiping his tears on the back of his hand, smiled. "Told you!"

"Complete response to therapy. No evidence of active lymphoma at this time." Dr. Keyes read the beautiful words aloud from the paper he held.

"Look at this." He turned, tapping on his computer. PET scan images slowly loaded, and Dr. Keyes guided us through the maze of blobs that meant absolutely nothing to me. Nodding as if they did, I couldn't stop smiling. *Remission!*

"We'll need to follow you every three months with blood work and every six months with a CT scan for the first year. Then we will gradually decrease the frequency as time goes by without recurrence," Dr. Keyes explained.

"Yeah, uh huh," I dumbly grinned. *Remission! Fiddler on the Roof's* song, "Tradition" played in my head with the word "remission" in its place: *Remission . . . remission . . . dum de de dum dum . . . REMISSION!*

". . . If it does come back, it won't matter if it's caught early or not as the treatment would be the same," Dr. Keyes shrugged.

My grin faded. "That would be the stem cell transplant?"

"Yes, that's right." Holding up his hands, Dr. Keyes added, "But I don't see that happening. You're going to be great! Even if you needed a stem cell, you would do fine. You're pretty tough." He chuckled.

"I can't thank you enough, Dr. Keyes. You've been a tremendous blessing, and I know your job has *got* to be hard." Daryl came to mind. "But you handle it well."

"It's patients like you that make it worthwhile." He smiled.

"Aww, thanks." I hugged him before we left.

As Jim drove home, I called Owen and Elyse with the wonderful news. "I'm in remission!"

Elyse shrieked, "Yay!" as Owen laughed in the background. After calling Mom and my siblings, I sent out dozens of text messages to friends across the island and across the country, giving them the wonderful news and thanking them for their prayers.

Oh, happy day!

God had made good on his promises of "*They will find nothing*" and "*You will be healed.*"

"We need to celebrate!" I announced to Jim.

"Yeah, we do!" He smiled at me. "Too bad I gotta go back to work now. Poor me . . ." Sticking out his lower lip, he playfully frowned at me.

"Just call in 'well.' Tell them you feel too good to go to work."

"I don't think so." He laughed, shaking his head.

At home, Owen and Elyse ran out to meet us in the garage, where we hugged and cried some more. The long, dark journey was over!

23

THE WRITE STUFF

The next month went by in a blur of trying to reestablish what normal looked like. After such a big event, I felt a little lost. What was I supposed to do now? I knew what I *wanted* to do.

I wanted to celebrate! Throw caution to the wind! Travel the world!

But there were still bills to be paid, laundry and dishes to be washed, and Elyse's schoolwork to grade. Jim's lunch needed to be made each morning, and Owen needed help with his college course work.

I was different, but life was the same.

Before my illness, Jim and I had both felt it was nearly time for me to return to work. Our savings had carried us through the years of homeschooling and now our home, vehicles, and appliances were showing their age.

After my illness, I wasn't so sure about returning to work. I longed to stay home with Elyse for her final year of high school and recover a bit more. Maybe grow in my hair. *Can't work wait until after she leaves for college?*

But a broken solar water-heating system, and a friend's offer of employment with a local nonprofit, changed my time frame. Praying on it, and with Jim's blessing, I applied for the job and was offered a full-time position. Flattered and a little stunned, I accepted.

Standing outside the office after the interview, I called home to share the news.

"Is that what you want, Mommy?" Elyse's voice broke.

"Oh Lilu. I wanted to be home with you until you graduated, but I guess this is God's plan for right now." My words hit her with a punch. How could she argue with "God's plan" if he was always right?

I quickly found full-time work absolutely exhausting. *How do normal moms do this?* Each morning when Jim and I left for work, Owen and Elyse were still fast asleep. Missing them, I'd leave love notes every morning and often called home on my lunch break.

Still, when we returned home, Elyse seldom smiled or spoke.

Helplessly, I watched Elyse struggling to finish her junior year of high school. Already several weeks behind after caring for me, she refused to turn in anything that wasn't done well. But she was too overwhelmed to do anything well.

While her online high school allowed flexibility, if she didn't complete the year soon, she'd have no summer break.

"Just *finish*," I pressed one evening. "Do one paper for one class, and you'll feel better. It doesn't have to be perfect."

Her tear-filled eyes broke my heart. "Oh Elyse," I said, holding her as she wept. "It's been a tough year, I know."

She needs me here.

"Jim, this just isn't working," I moaned the next morning. "Elyse is so sad. I'm worried."

"She'll get used to it," he said. "Lots of kids have moms that work."

"True, but she's been through a lot."

"She'll be fine." He shrugged. "She's a big girl."

On top of worries at home, I found that my immune system was nearly nonexistent. What began as a runny nose on Thursday developed into walking pneumonia by Saturday. Antibiotics cleared it, but my body was tired.

I found it hard to focus at work. There was always so much noise with people talking and moving around, phones ringing, and laughter. Sometimes I slipped into the bathroom just to breathe. *What was wrong with me?*

In the shower at night, I worried about relapse. Fear consumed any remaining strength after a long day. Forcing myself to keep moving, I tried to pray.

Wash your hair. *Lord, help me . . .* Rinse your hair. *God take away this fear . . .* Wet the bar of soap. *Jesus, you said I was healed . . .* Rub the washcloth . . . *Help me to believe . . .*

Exhausted, I crawled into bed only to repeat the routine the next day.

After several weeks of my absence, Elyse slept more and more. Her day began around lunchtime when she dragged herself out of bed. She ate, and then sat alone at the computer attempting her meaningless schoolwork.

One evening, when I returned home I found her slouched in her office chair, blankly staring at the computer screen.

"Hi, Lilu!" I set down my purse and lunch bag, forcing a tired smile. "How was your day?"

"The same." She scowled at me, turning back to the computer.

Shaking my head, I sighed. "We need to talk. Come," I ordered, taking her by the hand and pulling her to her room.

She sprawled on the bed and buried her face in her pillow as I shut the door. Sitting down beside her, I started rubbing her back.

"I don't know what's going on, Elyse, but I'm really worried about you."

Silence.

"God, help her through this and give me wisdom to know how to help," I whispered.

Her shoulders relaxed, then began to shake as sobs erupted. Tears ran down my face as I waited.

"When you were sick," she moaned, "I knew you'd get better. I held on, stayed cheerful, and took care of you. I waited for everything to go back to the way it was before you were sick." Her voice thickened as she sat up, facing me. "But then you went to work." The sobs grew with her words. "And this is worse than when you were ill. There is no end to this. Life will *never* be the same!"

"Oh Lilu . . ." I held her close as she sobbed in my arms. "I am so, so sorry." My heart sank. *Oh Jesus, I've abandoned her! I've dumped her for a stupid job.*

"I feel so selfish," she murmured, pulling away to reach for a tissue. "I know we need the money, and that I should be grateful, but I just feel so sad."

"You are NOT selfish. You are honest and human." Stroking her hair, I reached for a tissue of my own. "I'm so glad that you shared this with me. I don't like work either," I confessed. "Trust me; I want to be with you. I hate this too."

We sat quietly, without a solution.

"Must be Daddy's fault," I finally joked.

Elyse looked at me with red, swollen eyes, giggling, "Oh Moomy." It was the first glimmer of her old sparkling self that I'd seen in weeks.

Hugging her again, I whispered into her hair, "Thank you for being honest with me."

"Thank you for listening," she mumbled into my shoulder.

"We'll get through this somehow." I pulled back, holding her shoulders and looking into her eyes. "I love you more than I even know how to say."

"I love you too, Moomy."

Oh Jesus, I want to QUIT!

Over the next few days, Elyse and I came up with a doable plan to finish the prolonged school year. She also secured a student-helper position at the Makawao Library. The blessing of human contact with her wonderful coworkers, as well as a paycheck, made life's changes not quite so hard to take. For her anyway.

For me, my job was proving to be too much. The long hours, high expectation, and low pay of my payroll/accounts-payable position absolutely discouraged me. As I considered my employment, I came up with an algebraic equation to describe it:

$$[(Hardest\ Job\ Ever\ Done)^2] \times [(Pay\ Rate\ of\ Hardest\ Job) \div 2]$$
$$\times [Fear\ of\ no\ funding\ for\ next\ year] = Nonprofit\ Job$$

As the pressure mounted at work, I wondered if this really was God's plan for my life. Had he healed me for this? Being shut in my cubicle with spreadsheets, bills, time sheets, and deadlines didn't seem to convey my grateful heart. In fact, it sucked the joy out of living.

"What do you want me to do, God?" I asked one morning, kneeling against my old, brown chair.

"If you want me to continue working there, then I'll stay and do the best I can," I said. "I'll try not to look at my pay as my worth but remember that my worth comes from you." Finishing with quick prayers for our family and friends, I stood to prepare for another day.

As I turned toward the kitchen, one word was impressed upon my spirit:

"Write."

Pausing, I laughed. *Write?* But then excitement stirred.

When I was a child, my older sister Kathleen dragged me down Kokomo Road every other week, to the bookmobile parked beside Haiku Mart. Reading opened new worlds in our imagination, taking us far away from our tiny island life. Her passion fostered a love of books for me and a career as a librarian for her.

But write my own story? A decent Christmas letter was about the extent of my writing ability.

I didn't have time to dwell on it, though. I needed to get ready for work.

That evening, I wiped the dust off the cover of my neglected journal. Opening it to my last entry, I grimaced, seeing that I hadn't written a thing since I'd started working.

Where do I begin? An image of Snoopy atop his doghouse, pecking out "It was a dark and stormy night" on his typewriter came to mind.

Trying to concisely lay out all that had happened in written form, after a long day's work, or in between weekend chores, I found that my tired brain just couldn't string coherent words together.

"I can't write, Lord." On my knees after another failed attempt to focus and write, I gave up. "I'm too tired. I know you told me to do this, God, but I don't know how. I can't type fast enough. It's just too hard. I don't know what to do."

But I know what I don't want to do. I don't want to work!

Thinking about the recent loans we had made to replace a dying car and that broken solar water-heating unit, I calculated at least five more working years in my immediate future. And, with Jim talking about another loan for the huge start-up cost of a photovoltaic system, those five years would stretch into many more.

Frustrated, I knelt in silence, powerless to change the situation.

"*Ask me for provision.*" That same sweet, inaudible voice spoke once more.

Provision?

"Lord, please provide the strength I need to write," I began, searching for the right prayer. "Please keep me awake long enough to get something done."

That's not it.

"God, you can stretch hours into days. Can you stretch my days so I can get it all done? How about supernatural speed to do all that I want to do? Or a twenty-seven-hour day?"

Recognizing my sarcasm, I shook my head, trying again.

"Or better yet, can you provide a way for me to stay home and write?"

Home. That was it.

Immediately, doubts nagged at me. *Isn't it my duty to work? What about all the bills? Am I just super selfish?* But the idea had taken root. I thought back to Pastor Dale's sermon. I had finally found my dream.

That same week, a strange little envelope with the foreign postage arrived in my mailbox. Coincidence? Maybe. But I doubt it. The inheritance was already in the works when God told me to ask for provision. I could almost picture his smiling face, winking down at me from his heavenly throne.

I left work the week of Thanksgiving 2014. And what a glorious Thanksgiving it was!

After more than three years of reflection, tears, frustration, and prayer, I'm sitting at this old, plastic folding table, laptop whirring, laundry running, wondering how to close this story.

Looking outside, I see the afternoon sun, shining through the dirty window in front of me. Trees sway in breezy trade winds, the gutter rattles, and a monarch butterfly flutters by. It's another beautiful Maui day.

All my longing for change and my hungering for something more, and here I'd had what I sought all along. I love my home. I love being home. I love taking care of the people around me. What needed to change wasn't my location, husband, or finances. It was me.

How can I ever express my gratitude to God? He revealed the real me to me—flaws, mistakes, wrong thinking—and brought a deeper healing than cancer's cure.

EPILOGUE

Elyse finished high school on time and went on to graduate summa cum laude with her bachelor's degree from Oklahoma Baptist University. Her plans to continue her education, earn her doctorate in English, and become a college professor may have to wait. Rumor has it that she will be getting married later this year.

Owen earned an associate degree from the University of Hawaii Maui College and currently works in the garden center at The Home Depot. He drives himself to work every day, with a smile on his face, exceeding every expectation we'd hoped for him.

Brandon earned his doctorate in physical therapy and works in San Diego. Happily married to the love of his life, Kylie, they recently blessed us with our first grandchild, Noah. Another dream fulfilled.

Jim and I continue to grow in love for the Lord and for each other. I cannot thank God enough for this amazing man who allows me the freedom to be myself and to stay home. (And he still cooks for me!)

ACKNOWLEDGEMENTS

Lord Jesus, you've brought this book into being. Thank you for the journey and for revealing yourself to me in such a personal way. Please use this small offering for your glory.

Dale Gustafson, your Wide Awake sermon series stirred the wonder of dreaming and trusting Jesus as I'd never done before. Life's rainbows are much more vivid. Thank you.

Sylvia Frerking, you've asked to read this manuscript, punishing yourself through more versions than anyone else. Your enthusiasm means the world to me. Thank you.

Jen Hoke and **Norma Meis,** you two have been pillars of strength through homeschooling, illness, and life in general. Thank you.

Carla Bailey, when you bought that "Dragon" program for me, you not only made converting my journals to written form easier, but you believed in me. Thank you.

Katherine (Kaggy) Holdeman, your steadfast love of Jesus, prayers, pidgin skills, and patience with a nerd like me keep me laughing and moving forward. Mahalo planny.

Stephanie Mood, you were the very first person to read my initial writing attempts and your encouragement and guidance were a catalyst to its completion. Thank you.

Judy Morrow, your class at the Mt. Hermon Christian Writers Conference was an incredible blessing as is your continued friendship. Thank you.

Betty Evenson, how can I ever thank you enough for all the time on your couch reading through so many drafts? You've been my editing cheerleader and I thank you.

Susy Flory, you once told me that this was a story worth telling. Though you may not have realized it at the time, your words were a healing balm. Thank you.

Sarah Barnum, how can I ever thank you enough? You took my scattered story and rebuilt it into a story I'm happy to tell. Thank you.

Rebecca Miller, your careful attention to my many foibles and dangling modifiers didn't stop you from enjoying the narrative. Thank you for your kind words.

Mom, Gordon, Tess, Eleanor, Gary, and Kathleen, life's adventure is made better together with you. The old stories we've shared, laughed, and cried through, as well as the many prayers on my behalf, are very precious to me. I thank God for each one you.

To the many friends who have prayed, brought meals, offered hugs, mileage, and support, I cannot thank you enough. Mahalo Ke Akua, thank you Almighty God, for all of these.

Made in the USA
Monee, IL
30 June 2021